Great Christians

GREAT CHRISTIANS

Their Response and Witness

by CATHERINE HERZEL

Illustrated by HAROLD MINTON

GUSTAV K. WIENCKE, *Editor*

Lutheran Church Press, Philadelphia

LCA Sunday Church School Series

This pupil's Reader is accompanied by a pupil's Workbook, *Great Christians,* and by a Teacher's Guide. This material has been prepared for use in Term 1 in the Sunday church school (5-1.) The general theme for the year is "Our Christian Response and Witness."

ABOUT THIS BOOK

NINETEEN CENTURIES HAVE PASSED since Jesus sent his disciples out to preach the good news of the kingdom of God and since the Christian church began. In all those hundreds of years there have been men and women who have loved Jesus and served him gladly. Men and women were called to do difficult and brave things for Christ, their Savior. Many of them gave their lives freely in loving obedience to Christ.

We owe much to the great Christians of the past and of the present. They have helped to build the Christian church. They have guarded the faith in dangerous and troubled times.

Most of all, they help us to think about what it means to be a Christian. They call us to join in their company—the great communion of saints—and to witness to our faith. We may not be called to die in an arena as did Polycarp or to travel to distant parts of the world as did Laubach, but we are called to serve and love Jesus Christ wherever we are.

Contents

PART I

Heroes When the Church Was Young

I. Polycarp

TO LIVE AND DIE FOR CHRIST

MOST OF THE TIME Smyrna was a peaceful city. Christians and non-Christians lived side by side in the white houses that climbed the hills and looked down on the harbor. But in the last few weeks things had changed. The people in Smyrna had begun to mutter and complain:

"These Christians do not worship our emperor."

"They do not serve the ancient gods."

"They follow strange and different customs."

In A.D. 155,Smyrna, like the rest of Asia Minor, was ruled by Rome. In fact, the Roman emperor ruled most of the known world. He was worshiped as a god. Anyone who refused to worship him was considered a traitor.

The people of Smyrna could not understand the Christians. Why should anyone refuse to worship the emperor? It was such a simple thing to do. People began to fear and then to hate the stubborn followers of this strange religion. Soldiers began to hunt out Christians and drag them before the Roman magistrates.

"Drop a pinch of incense on the fire as a sacrifice to the emperor, our god," the judge would command. "Say the oath 'By our Lord, the emperor!'"

To non-Christians this seemed as harmless as pledging allegiance to the flag seems to us. But Christians knew that there is only one Lord. Saying the Roman oath was one way of breaking the First Commandment.

"We have no other Lord but Jesus Christ," they would protest. "We cannot sacrifice to the emperor."

"Just one pinch of incense," the Roman judge would insist. "Everyone else does it."

"We cannot," the Christians would reply.

The verdict was always the same. "Away with them. Take them to the arena. They are traitors—all of them."

A Last Prayer

The Christians in Smyrna were especially proud of their bishop, or chief pastor—a man named Polycarp. Polycarp was one of the last men alive who had known one of the disciples of Jesus. He had known John, the apostle. When he was a boy he had also talked with other men who had followed Jesus.

Soon the government officials began searching for Poly-carp, the leader of the Christians. Some of the bishop's friends sent him to live in a farmhouse outside the city. They thought that he would be safe there.

One day a young man named Justin came bursting into the farmhouse. He gasped out his message:

"They're coming. . . . They're coming! They know . . . that Bishop Polycarp . . . is here! They captured two of the bishop's servants and tortured them. One of them broke down. They are coming out here. I am not much ahead of them. Warn the bishop!"

The owner of the farmhouse hurried upstairs to the bishop's room. When Polycarp heard the news, he said quietly, "God's will be done. I will not flee any further or put your lives in any more danger."

Even while the two men were talking, they heard dogs barking outside. Horses neighed and men were shouting. The soldiers had come.

"Where is he?" a rough voice demanded. "Here, you," the officer said, dragging in the slave who had told where Polycarp was hiding. "Which one is Polycarp?"

A door opened. "Here I am," the bishop said. "Are you looking for me?"

The officer let the slave go. "Yes," he growled.

"You have had a hard march. You must be hungry and thirsty," said Polycarp. "Bring some food for these men."

The officer started to speak. This was not what he had expected. Then he sat down quietly at the table.

"I have one request," Polycarp said. "Give me one hour so that I can pray for those I love."

"You may have that," said the officer.

Polycarp went back to his room and sank to his knees. Thoughts about his church and his people rushed into his heart and mind. He began to pray, asking God to shelter them.

Witness in the Arena

The arena was a popular place in Smyrna. Chariot races were held there. Athletic contests took place there. Sometimes crowds gathered to watch gladiators fight to the death against each other or against fierce, hungry lions.

In the arena the crowd was waiting for a bloody sight. They wanted to see the Christians face the wild beasts. "Bring in the Christians," the crowd shouted. "Throw the traitors to the beasts!"

The trumpets blew and the crowd fell silent. A little group of Christians was pushed out into the arena. Then the doors of the animal cages were opened. The lions rushed out into the bright sunlight. The sight of the lions was too much for Quintus. He screamed and stumbled to the place where the Roman governor, Lucius Statius Quadratus, sat.

"I'll say the oath—I'll offer incense," Quintus cried.

The governor nodded. Soldiers came forward and led the man out of the arena—from death to safety.

But the other Christians remained firm even when the lions started across the arena toward them. If they shook with fear, they had only to look at young Germanicus. He faced death without a sign of weakness. Their courage rose again.

It was soon over. The unarmed Christians were no match for the angry lions.

The crowd was still not satisfied. "Where is the leader of the Christians?" they shouted. "Where is Polycarp? Throw him to the lions."

Others took up the cry, "Polycarp! Polycarp!"

"There he is!" shouted a man as he saw the old bishop. Soldiers were bringing Polycarp to the Roman governor. The mob burst into shouts and jeers.

The governor was calm. He paid no attention to the shouting crowd. He looked kindly at Polycarp.

"Think of your age," he said. "Change your mind. All you have to do is swear 'By the Fortune of Caesar!' Then I will set you free." The governor wanted to make things easy for the thin old man.

Polycarp shook his head.

The Roman governor persisted. "Take the oath. Curse Christ and I will let you go."

Polycarp looked straight at the Roman governor. The old man seemed to grow taller as he spoke.

"Eighty-six years I have served him, and he has never done me any wrong. How can I curse my King who has saved me?"

Finally the governor saw that he could not persuade Polycarp to change his mind. He gave the signal to the herald. The herald marched into the arena before the crowd and faced the north. "Polycarp has proclaimed himself to be a Christian," he shouted.

Then he faced the east: "Polycarp has proclaimed himself to be a Christian."

He faced the south and then the west. Each time he announced the same thing.

The crowd roared its hatred. But the soldiers did not place Polycarp before the lions. Instead, they led him to a stake where he was to be burned to death. They tied him securely. Before the fire was lit, Polycarp looked up into the blue sky and prayed:

"Lord God Almighty, Father of thy beloved and blessed Servant Jesus Christ . . . I bless thee because thou hast deemed me worthy of this day and hour to take my part in the number of the martyrs. . . . For this and for everything I praise thee, I bless thee, I glorify thee. . . . Amen."

A Christian who heard Polycarp's prayer and saw all that happened wrote down the story of Polycarp's death. The church in Smyrna sent the story in a letter, or epistle, to another church. From church to church the epistle from Smyrna was passed along. All over the Roman Empire, Christians read the brave words of Bishop Polycarp: "Eighty-six years I have served him, and he has never done me any wrong. How can I curse my King who has saved me?"

2. Witness in the Copper Mines

UNNAMED CHRISTIANS

THE YEAR 304 was one that Christians long remembered with shivers of fear. That was the year of the Great Persecution. This was not like the persecution when Polycarp was burned at the stake. At that time, Christians were hunted out in only a few places like Smyrna and for only a short time. But in the year 304 the Roman emperor Diocletian (di-o-*klee*-shan) issued a series of laws against Christians in all parts of the empire. This soldier-emperor did this because he wanted to unite his empire. He wanted everyone to worship the ancient gods of the Romans. He wanted to crush Christianity as a strange, new religion which might divide his empire. Christian churches were to be destroyed; Christian writings were to be burned; Christians were to be seized and imprisoned.

In this year of persecution there were many men and women who suffered and died for their faith. Many of these heroes were ordinary people—farmers and fishermen, free men and slaves. Their names are no longer known because they were not as famous as Bishop Polycarp. This is a story about two whom we will call Cornelius and Marcus. It is a story that shows how Christians witnessed during the Great Persecution.

Cornelius was a tall, weatherbeaten fisherman who lived in the harbor town of Gaza in southern Palestine. With him was young, curly-haired Marcus. Both were far from home and the two men seemed like two tiny specks in the wide and rocky desert. They had been walking to the south for several days.

As they walked, Cornelius thought about his brother and his friends. What would he have done if he had been at home when the soldiers had come? What would he have said? Would he have had courage to declare his faith?

Marcus stopped for a moment and wiped the sweat from his forehead. The glare of the sun on the treeless sand was blinding. "How much farther do we have to go?" he asked.

"A day or a day and a half at the most," Cornelius answered encouragingly. He was just as tired as Marcus, but he was determined to go on.

"When I think of our friends . . ." Marcus began. He paused for a moment. "We are free men; they are slaves. It's hard enough for us to keep going across this terrible wasteland. What must it have been like for them, with soldiers pushing them on day after day? Then to be forced to work in the copper mines!"

The two men plodded on for some time, saying nothing. Then Marcus burst out, "To think that the soldiers took them all—the women and the children, too."

"If they had been criminals . . ." Cornelius sighed. "But all they did was meet and listen to God's Word."

Marcus shifted the small package of food he carried on his back. There was one question that kept bothering him. "We live in a strange world," he said finally. "Why do good people—like our friends in the mines—have to suffer while the wicked live easy, comfortable lives?"

Cornelius was older and wiser, but he had no answer. "I've often asked myself that question," he admitted. "It's hard to understand . . . maybe we can never understand why the world is as it is . . . but we do know that God is with us. He has not forgotten you or me or your father or my brother or the others in the copper mines."

A Secret Sign

As the two men neared the mountains and the copper mines, they checked their plans. Marcus was the bold one, but Cornelius was older and wiser. He knew the great risk they were taking.

"Marcus," he advised, "we must be on the alert every minute. The guards must not know that we are visiting the Christians in the mines, or we will be in danger. I have heard about other Christians who tried to help their friends in the mines. They were captured before they even got to these hills. The guards blinded each of them in one eye and crippled them so that they could not run away. Then they forced them to work in the mines with the others. We must be careful so that we can remain free and help the Christians who have already been captured."

Marcus shuddered. "I know it is dangerous," he said. "I will be careful."

Late in the afternoon, the two men cautiously climbed the last hill and looked down on the mining camp below.

They had come this far safely. They dared not risk being seen now. Quietly they crept into the bushes just below the crest of the hill to wait for nightfall. While they waited, Cornelius found a piece of broken pottery and scratched the sign of a fish on it. Then he put it into his pocket.

Finally the sudden darkness of desert nightfall came. Still the two men lay hidden in the bushes. Gradually the mining camp quieted down. The guards were silent. Slowly and cautiously, Cornelius crept down the hillside to the nearest hut. Quietly he tossed the piece of broken pottery into the hut. He heard it rattle as it fell. There was a long silence—then the sound of someone moving toward the fragment. Cornelius imagined someone holding the piece of pottery toward the flickering lamp to see the mark on it.

Cornelius waited, but all was silent.

"Who are you?" The question came so quietly and so unexpectedly that Cornelius was startled. He looked into the shadows behind him and saw a man.

"Cornelius from Gaza," he whispered back.

For a moment everything was still. Then the unknown man in the shadows said slowly, "I name as Lord . . ." He waited for Cornelius to finish.

"Jesus the Christ," answered Cornelius.

The dark figure reached out his hand and grasped Cornelius in a friendly way. "Listen!" he whispered. "The Gaza Christians live in a hut on the far side of the camp. You cannot possibly get to them safely from here. But when the moon rises, Christians from all over the camp will slip into the shed next to ours for prayer and worship. You can see your friends there."

"You use the shed as a church?" whispered Cornelius.

"Yes," answered the man in the shadows. "When we first built these huts, we built an extra storage shed. Often we gather there after the day's work for prayer and worship. The guards know about it, but so far they have said nothing. They pretend that it is just a storage shed."

Witness at the Mines

Cornelius crawled back up the hillside to Marcus and told him the news. The two men lay together in their hiding place, waiting for the moon to rise. Soon the moon appeared over the horizon. Dim figures appeared in the valley below and began moving silently across the camp to the shed. Quietly Cornelius and Marcus climbed down the hillside and entered the low building with the others.

"Cornelius!" It was only a whisper, but the arms around his shoulders were real and pressed him hard.

"Gaius, my brother!" Cornelius hugged his brother and felt the thin shoulders under his tunic. Marcus had found his father. The two could hardly keep their voices down.

"Is our mother still alive? Still free?" asked Gaius.

"She is," answered Cornelius. "She prays for you and sends this gift."

Cornelius reached inside his tunic and brought out a soft leather pouch. "Herbs and medicine," he explained as he handed it to Gaius. "Use it for the old and the sick."

Then he drew out a long thin roll. "And a scroll—a copy of two letters of Paul," he said. "Your friend made a copy for you."

Gaius was so happy that he could not speak. His arms held Cornelius in a tighter grasp.

The light at the door was darkened as two men appeared. They bent their heads and entered, leading an old, old man. He was blind, and lame in one leg.

"That is John, our lector. He knows many words of Holy Scripture and repeats them for us," Gaius whispered.

The old, blind man stood in front of the group and began to recite the words of the First Epistle of Peter:

"Blessed be the God and Father of our Lord Jesus Christ! By his great mercy we have been born anew to a living hope through the resurrection of Jesus Christ from the dead, and to an inheritance which is imperishable. . . .

"In this you rejoice, though now for a little while you may have to suffer various trials, so that the genuineness of your faith, more precious than gold which though perishable is tested by fire, may redound to praise and glory and honor at the revelation of Jesus Christ."

Cornelius looked on in wonder. It was hard to believe that the old man was not reading from a roll of papyrus as Christians had done in the church at Gaza.

Cornelius forgot the long hot trip across the desert. He forgot how hungry he was. It was good to be with Christian brothers.

Suddenly the first man to whom Cornelius had spoken came to his side. He put his mouth close to Cornelius' ear.

"The guards seem to suspect that strangers are here," he whispered. "They may come to check on who is here. If they find you, they will make you slaves. Come with me. I will help you get away."

Cornelius said a hurried goodbye to his brother. Then he tugged at the sleeve of Marcus. "Come on," he whispered. "We've got to go."

The two men followed their guide out into the shadows between the sheds.

At the edge of the camp, the three men stopped.

"God go with you," the guide said. "May he bless you for coming to see us. Ask our Christian brothers to pray for us. Tell them that even here in the copper mines God is with us. We are winning new believers. He gives us strength and peace and courage. We will never betray him."

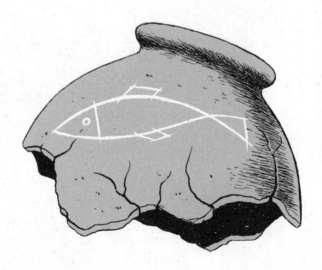

3. Athanasius

THIS I BELIEVE

HUNDREDS OF PEOPLE poured out of the large domed church in the city of Alexandria in Egypt. "Arius is right. His teachings are true," someone shouted.

"Arius is old. His teachings are false," called another.

Athanasius, a young deacon in the church of Alexandria, pushed his way through the crowd. All the way home he thought about the sermon he had just heard.

"Arius is an old and wise man," he thought. "He explains the Christian faith so forcefully that thousands come to hear him. But he teaches that God created Jesus Christ, as if Jesus were some kind of second-class god. He teaches that Jesus was not really God and not really man, but a kind of heroic being in between.

"I know that Arius is wrong. Our God is One, and yet Jesus Christ is not some kind of lower god."

Soon the discussion between the old teacher in Alexandria and the young deacon spread throughout the Roman Empire. Some of the leaders of the church believed that

Arius was right—that Jesus was a kind of lesser god. Others
defended Athanasius, who believed that Jesus was truly
equal with God.

Emperor Constantine became worried about all the
quarreling. He had granted special favors to Christians
because he had hoped that Christianity would help to
keep his empire together. Now it seemed that the debate
among the leaders of the church would split the empire
into dozens of smaller parts. Something had to be done.
Constantine decided to invite all the Christian bishops to
come together for a meeting in his palace at Nicaea.

Council of Nicaea

The year was 325. Christian bishops from all over the
world had come to Nicaea for the first gathering of all the
leaders of the Christian church. With them came Arius,
the famous teacher, and Athanasius, who was secretary
for one of the bishops of Alexandria.

Under the urging of Emperor Constantine, the bishops
at the council of Nicaea drew up a creed or statement of
belief. This creed was adopted by the council and came to
be called the Nicene Creed. In this creed the leaders of the
church took sides against Arius. The creed stated plainly
that Jesus is "Very God of Very God, Begotten, not made."

Because Arius refused to agree to this statement of
belief, Emperor Constantine banished him.

But the quarrel was not over. Arius was a popular man
and an excellent speaker. At the council, Emperor Constantine had been able to force the bishops to agree to one
point of view. But when the bishops returned to their own
churches, the quarrel began all over again. Was Christ

ΠΙΣΤΕΥΟΜΕΝ ΕΙΣ ΕΝΑ
ΘΕΟΝ ΠΑΤΕΡΑ ΠΑΝΤΟ
ΚΡΑΤΟΡΑ ΠΟΗΤΗΝ
ΟΥΡΑΝΟΥ ΚΑΙ ΓΗΣ

really God, or was he a kind of lesser god? Bishop argued against bishop. The council had really settled nothing.

Arrival in Tyre

In the year 335 Emperor Constantine summoned the bishops to a meeting in the city of Tyre. This time he was sure he could get some kind of agreement.

Athanasius was now the strongest defender of the Nicene Creed. The bishops who agreed with Arius decided that if Athanasius could be gotten out of the way, the teachings of Arius would triumph in the church.

Down at the harbor of Tyre, great crowds had gathered to watch the ships come in. Everyone wanted to see the Christian bishops as they arrived for the council.

"That's Bishop Eusebius," shouted a man in the crowd, pointing to one of the men who sided with Arius.

"There's the ship from Egypt. Let's see the Egyptian bishops," said a tall, thin man, pushing through the crowd.

There was a murmur, then a hush as two elderly men stepped from the ship. Each was blind in one eye! They had been in prison during the Great Persecution. Some in the crowd fell to their knees as the elderly men walked by.

"Where's Athanasius? Which one is he?" others called.

People jostled each other as they tried to see Athanasius, who was now the Bishop of Alexandria. They had heard about this bishop who was ready to defy the whole council of bishops—even the emperor—for his faith.

Plot Against Athanasius

Bishop Eusebius took charge of the assembly of bishops. He sat on the chief bishop's throne, ready to defend the beliefs of Arius. Around him in rows sat the other bishops. Many wore rich robes embroidered with gold.

Eusebius began the assembly by saying that there was one matter that must be taken care of immediately. The Bishop of Alexandria—he glared at Athanasius—had been accused of arranging the murder of one of his own bishops, a man named Arsenius. Not only that, but the Bishop of Alexandria—another pointed stare—had been accused of cutting off the hand of the dead man so that he could use it for black magic. Such terrible accusations must be answered here and now.

Athanasius stood up to make his defense. He had been warned that this charge would be made against him. He was ready to defend himself. "Does anyone in this assembly know Arsenius by sight?" he asked boldly.

"Yes," called several voices. Many heads nodded in agreement. Athanasius turned toward the doorway and signaled to his friends. A tall man draped in a long cloak walked slowly toward the center of the hall. A thick, dark hood covered his head and face.

"Lift up your head; face these men," Athanasius said.

The man raised his head. His hood fell back, and he stood face to face with the assembly.

"It is Arsenius," whispered an onlooker.

"Arsenius!" murmured the bishops.

Athanasius reached toward the man in the cloak. He pushed back one sleeve of the man's cloak and held the man's arm high in the air. Then, grasping the man's other hand, he brought both hands into view.

"I don't suppose God has given more than two hands to any man, not even to Arsenius," he said dryly.

The plot against Athanasius seemed to have fallen apart. But Bishop Eusebius was not to be defeated so easily. He knew the superstitions of the crowd who had gathered.

"It's magic!" he cried out quickly. "Athanasius works magic. This is not Arsenius we see, but an illusion."

"Come on," said a friend to Athanasius, "we must get out of here before the crowd goes wild."

Athanasius and five of his bishops escaped from the hall. They hurried down to the harbor and boarded a ship for Constantinople.

At the council, meanwhile, the enemies of Athanasius persuaded the bishops to declare Athanasius unworthy to be a bishop.

Exile to Europe

One day as Emperor Constantine was riding through the streets of Constantinople, a strange figure appeared in his path. The emperor reined in his horse.

"Take him away," he ordered his guards.

"I am Athanasius, Bishop of Alexandria," said the man firmly, "and I ask justice from my emperor."

Constantine was impressed by the bishop's courage. He agreed to listen to his story. When the emperor had heard Athanasius' charges, he called the men who had accused him to Constantinople.

Only Eusebius came, but he was wise enough to drop the story of the murder of Arsenius. He had a new accusation.

"Athanasius wants power," he said to the emperor. "He is planning to buy all the wheat in Egypt and stop grain ships from leaving Alexandria. Rome will starve."

Athanasius tried to defend himself. He tried to show how absurd it was that a poor man could buy so much wheat. But the emperor would not listen. He did not understand what these two men were really arguing about. To him Athanasius was just a stubborn troublemaker. He ordered Athanasius exiled far away in Europe.

The quarrel between those who believed as Arius did—that Christ was a kind of half-god—and those who believed as Athanasius did—that Christ was both true God and true man—went on for many years. Constantine died and his three sons fought for the empire. Their quarrel over the empire became involved with the quarrels of the followers of Arius and Athanasius. Whenever the followers of Arius gained power, they banished all the bishops who followed Athanasius. Whenever the followers of Athanasius were in power, they banished all the bishops who were followers of Arius.

Witness in Time of Danger

In the year 356, Athanasius was in Alexandria as bishop for a short time. On the night of February eighth, he was conducting an all-night worship service to help people prepare to receive Holy Communion the next day. The huge church was crowded with worshipers.

Suddenly fierce yells were heard outside the church. A frightened messenger hurried inside to announce that the emperor had sent a large company of soldiers to capture the bishop. Athanasius asked a deacon to read Psalm 136.

The deacon began reading softly: "O give thanks to the Lord, for he is good."

The people replied with the next words of the psalm: "For his steadfast love endures for ever."

The deacon's trembling voice grew stronger. He read on through the psalm which tells how God saved his people from their enemies in Egypt.

". . . to him who smote great kings." The words rang out in the great church. The people replied with one voice: "For his steadfast love endures for ever."

Finally the doors of the church crashed open. Soldiers rushed into the sanctuary with their swords drawn. People shrieked and pushed their way out of the church. In the confusion that followed, some of Athanasius' friends hurried him out into the safety of the dark night.

Final Triumph

In his lifetime, Athanasius was exiled five times, and five times he was restored as Bishop of Alexandria. Even in exile he kept the battle alive for the Christian faith as stated in the Nicene Creed. At last in the year 366 he returned, and the people welcomed him in triumph. The battle had been won for the Nicene Creed. Throughout the Christian world, Athanasius became known as the man who stood like a rock for his faith in Jesus Christ.

4. Boniface

SHARING THE GOSPEL

"Get me a sharp axe," said Boniface to his servant. "The biggest axe you can find."

"An axe for the bishop," muttered the servant. He could not understand. "Why would Bishop Boniface want an axe?"

"Wear your finest robes," said Boniface to the priests. "Dress as you would for a great festival."

The priests could not understand the orders of Bishop Boniface either. Here they were in a muddy village deep in the forests of Germany. There were no big churches here. There were no great cities. Around them in the dark woods lived pagan tribes who worshiped Thor, the god of thunder, and Odin and Freya, and many other gods.

Because the priests trusted and loved Boniface, they obeyed. But they could not help wondering what was going to happen that day.

It was in the year 734 when the strange procession entered the forests of tall pine and fir trees. First marched

men carrying bright silk flags. Then came the priests in long robes of white and red. The priests swung silver pots of smoking incense to and fro. The fragrant smoke spread into the dark woods. People hiding behind the trees and bushes could smell it and see the bright procession. In the midst of the procession strode Boniface. His robe glittered with gold and silver. In his hand he carried a tall cross. Behind him walked his servant with a big iron axe.

News spread swiftly. "What is going on?" asked the German people of the forests. "These people are not like the other Christians we have seen."

The only other Christians the forest people had seen were humble Irish monks who wore rough clothing and worked quietly in monasteries which they had built with their own hands. Boniface was different. The forest people

could not help but notice Boniface. Now he was planning
to do something that would make their blood run cold.

The procession marched straight toward the biggest
tree in the forest. It was a mighty oak, the holy tree of the
god Thor. Here the German people of the forest brought
their sacrifices. Here they worshiped Thor.

The banners, the chanting priests, the noble Boniface
came to a halt before the great oak. Boniface waited quietly. From their hiding places in the tangled underbrush
the people of the forest watched Boniface with angry, fear-
ful eyes.

"If he touches that tree, Thor will strike him down with
a thunderbolt!" whispered an old man confidently. A few
crept out of the woods to watch.

The servant handed Boniface the heavy iron axe. Boniface raised it high and struck a crashing blow against the
tree. The frightened tribesmen ran back into the forest, ex-
pecting the sky to rumble with angry thunder.

Again and again the axe bit into the tree. Finally the tree
began to sway. It shuddered for a moment and then cracked
and fell at Boniface's feet, splitting into four great pieces.

Boniface stood unharmed. The terrified forest people
crept toward the clearing. They were still frightened, but
they wondered why the great Thor had not defended his
holy tree against this Christian bishop.

"Cut this tree into boards," ordered Boniface.

He paced off a spot. "Here we will build a chapel. Where
men once worshiped Thor, they will gather to worship
God and learn to love and serve Jesus Christ."

When the great oak tree fell, the pagan faith of the German tribes fell with it. From village to village the news

spread about the bishop with the tall cross and the terrible
axe.

Great Missionary to Germany

Boniface had been born in the southern part of England
some time between 672 and 675. He became a monk because he loved the church and because he loved books. As
a young English monk he might easily have become a great
scholar or even the head of a monastery. But Boniface felt
that God was calling him to a different life. Across the English Channel lived many tribes and peoples who knew
nothing about Christianity. Boniface dreamed of going to
them as a missionary.

Finally the abbot of the monastery consented. "You may
go to Frisia, and God be with you!"

Frisia was a country near the mouth of the Rhine River
where the city of Utrecht stands today. Boniface started
out with high hopes, but he soon had to turn back to England. There was savage fighting among the tribes in Frisia.
No one would listen to a missionary.

Boniface did not give up. A few years later he was sent
to the lands of Hesse and Thuringia, east of the Rhine
River where Germany is today. Here lived tribes which
worshiped sacred oak trees and springs and rocks. When
the moon was full, they gathered for strange rites in forest
and field. What was worse, some of the tribesmen who had
long ago become Christians had slipped back into heathen
ways.

As Boniface went deeper into the German forests he
found "the most savage people of Germany," people who
still sacrificed human beings to the gods of blood and war.

Boniface traveled boldly through these dangerous forests. Everywhere he went he preached, baptized, overturned idols, and built little wooden chapels. He knew that people needed to see as well as hear. That is why he carried flags and wore bright robes.

Building the Church

From the forests of Germany Boniface wrote many letters to his friends in England. "Pray for me," he wrote. "Pray that God can use even the work of a sinner like me." Friends sent him gifts of linens for a chapel altar and the books he loved so well.

More than that, some of Boniface's friends came to join him and to help in the work in the forests of Germany. One was a young nun named Lioba (lee-*o*-ba), who was related to Boniface. She had known Boniface long ago when she was a child and had written to him, sending him verses which she timidly asked him to correct. Now that she was grown up, she was eager to join him in Germany and have a part in his great missionary work. Four other nuns came with Lioba. Boniface helped them build several convents along the Main River.

In the year 732 the pope asked Boniface to come to Rome. "I shall make you an archbishop. Your field shall be all of Germany. Go where you wish to go. Help build the church. Spread the gospel of Christ the Savior!"

This was the work that Boniface loved. He did not stay in an archbishop's palace. Instead he traveled through the southern part of Germany and chose new bishops to help him take care of the new churches in that land. As a result, all of Germany was gathered into one Christian church.

Times were not always peaceful. Sometimes pagan tribes attacked the Christian settlements. In one series of raids they robbed and burned thirty churches. Boniface worked hard to rebuild the damage.

Witness to the End

When Boniface was an old man he did not choose to retire to a place of peace and safety. He remembered the Frisians, whom he had worked with long ago. They were among the wildest and most dangerous tribes in the forests. Boniface wanted to go back once more to his work as a pioneer missionary.

In the spring of 754, when the ice had melted from the rivers and the snow had disappeared from the forest paths, Boniface traveled northward. He knew that he might never return.

First he went to the Borne River. There he was to meet a large group of newly baptized converts. "Come and confirm us and give us your blessing," a message had said.

When Boniface reached the river and camped there, all seemed peaceful. Then, just before dawn on the fifth of June, heathen tribes attacked the camp.

"Do not fight," Boniface called to those who wanted to defend him. "We are bidden not to return evil for evil, but good for evil."

As the tribesmen slashed at him with swords, Boniface held a copy of the Gospel high over his head. Even though he was killed, his work was carried on by his followers.

To this day the gospel book which Boniface treasured is still kept in a church at Fulda in Germany. There one can still see the pages, cut by the swords of long ago.

PART II

Renewers of the Church

5. Francis of Assisi

BROTHER TO ALL

"CAN'T YOU TALK some sense into him?" sputtered the rich Italian merchant. "I tell you, my son has gone out of his mind! Do you know what he has done? He has sold his horse and a bolt of my best cloth. He is giving the money to beggars. He says he is serving a new master, Jesus."

The rich merchant from the city of Assisi in central Italy sputtered and fumed as he pleaded with his bishop.

The bishop listened carefully to the merchant's story. He knew that the man wanted his son Francis to become a knight. He also knew that Francis had grown up as the favorite son in a rich and elegant home.

"Let's talk to your son," the bishop said.

The three men met together—the angry father, the bishop, and cheerful, young Francis. "Let it be in public," said Francis. So the three went to the market place.

The bishop watched as Francis bowed to his father. The boy did not seem to be crazy. First Francis gave his father his purse—all the money he had gotten for selling his horse.

Then the young man took off his fine cloak and rich garments. He handed them to his father. The bishop looked on approvingly, and then gave Francis his own cloak.

Francis had given up parties and gay times. He had decided to leave his father's fine home. A great change had come over him. He had taken to heart the words of Jesus:

Go, sell what you have, and give to the poor, . . . and come, follow me (Mark 10:21).

Francis wanted to serve Jesus in complete poverty. But how? First he went among the beggars and lepers in the city of Assisi and tried to help them. Then he went out to the nearby countryside and began rebuilding the country churches which had been allowed to fall into ruins. He dressed in the rough brown clothing of the poor people and worked with his hands. He shared whatever he had with anyone who needed help. At first people laughed at this strange young man.

After a time, however, a famous nobleman came to join Francis in his work. Then came a learned man of the church; then a poor laborer. The three men worked joyfully with Francis. They toiled in the fields with the farmers. They shared what little they had with the poor. They sang together. They tried to obey the words of Jesus:

Preach as you go, saying, "The kingdom of heaven is at hand." Heal the sick, . . . cleanse lepers, cast out demons. You received without pay, give without pay. Take no gold, nor silver, nor copper in your belts, no bag for your journey, nor two tunics, nor sandals, nor a staff; for the laborer deserves his food (Matthew 10:7-10).

These words came to be called the "Rule of Francis."

Witness of Barefoot Brothers

As Francis went about helping others, he discovered that most people were greedy for money. They wanted to live in comfort with plenty of food to eat and good homes to live in. They did not care what happened to anyone but themselves. Even priests and monks and bishops lived in luxury. The leaders of the church were not ready or willing to help the poor. Francis felt that Christ had called him to serve others and to live without owning anything. He would serve "Lady Poverty."

As he went about helping others, Francis decided that he must give himself completely to preaching this simple message: Men must repent of their sins and live in love with their fellow men. They must learn to help the poor.

Francis and his followers traveled barefooted about the countryside preaching this message. They traveled two by two, preaching and singing and helping. Because they did not live hidden away from the world in rich monasteries, Francis' followers called themselves friars, or brothers. They tried to be brothers to the whole world.

Many bishops and other leaders of the church thought that Francis' ideas were very foolish. They jeered at the poor friars dressed in brown peasants' cloth. They turned away in disgust from the sick and the crippled. Because Francis was not ordained, they thought they could laugh at him. The church had not even given him permission to go about preaching and teaching.

In the year 1210 the pope gave Francis official permission to continue his preaching and teaching among the poor. Now many came to join the band of poor friars. They

sang and worked as they went about the countryside helping the poor. They preached the gospel to the poor and
sick whom the church seemed to have forgotten. Because
of the friars' work, people were strengthened in their faith,
and the church itself was refreshed and renewed.

Rich and powerful church leaders, poor farmers, rob-
bers in the forest—Francis treated them all as brothers.
Even the animals responded to the love of Francis. Once
Francis met a boy who had trapped some doves and was
taking them to market. The boy offered them to Francis,
who took them gladly—not for an evening meal, but so that
he could give them back their freedom. He set the birds
free near his chapel. They stayed near the chapel as if they
knew that this was a house of safety.

"If I could speak to the emperor," Francis said one time,
"I would ask him to make a law that no one be allowed to
harm our sister the Lark." (The emperor, Frederick II,
was a great hunter.) "And I would celebrate Christmas by
having the mayors of the towns and the lords of the castles

and villages order men to throw wheat and other grain outside for the birds. And in reverence for Christ, who rested
in the manger between an ox and an ass, owners of these
animals should provide the best fodder for them."

Witness Before the Sultan

In the year 1219 a great and terrible war raged between
Christians and Moslems. Vast Christian armies gathered
in Europe and sailed east to try to capture the Holy Land
from the Moslems. Francis sailed along with the armies
from Europe. He believed that it would be more Christlike
to preach the gospel peacefully to the Moslems than to
beat them down with swords and battering rams and fire.
Francis set out to visit the Sultan of Egypt, one of the Moslem leaders, and to speak to him in peace.

As Francis and his companion neared the palace of the
sultan, Brother Illuminatio whispered, "The guards look
dangerous. Don't you think we should turn back? If the
guards guess that we are Christians, there will be no time
for you to talk to them about peace and love. Their curved
swords will do their work before you can say a thing."

But Francis was unafraid. He walked forward calmly.
When the guards saw him, they drew their swords. They
held their great curved blades ready as they listened to
this little man. Probably they could not understand the
words he spoke. But they did like the friendly look in his
eyes. The guards were puzzled by these two strange men
on foot. Moslems believed that fools or lunatics were under
the special care of Allah—as the Moslems call God. Perhaps the guards respected these two as strange fools, protected by Allah himself.

Even when Francis tried to explain that he wanted to see the sultan, the guards did not use their glittering curved swords. Instead they took him to their superior officer. Francis was handed along from one officer to another until he finally stood in the very presence of the sultan himself.

What happened when these two men met is not known. We do know that the sultan was a mighty warrior, defending his homeland against the invading crusaders. We can be sure that the gentle Francis talked about the Christian faith. And since the sultan treated Francis kindly, he must have respected the love and the pure heart of the brown-robed monk. At any rate, the sultan did dismiss Francis peacefully and allowed him to go back in safety.

Witness with a Happy Heart

When Francis came home from his long and dangerous journey to the sultan, he was saddened by what he found. His band of "little brothers," who had started out in complete poverty, now lived in a fine stone building. Their little band had become a rich and complicated organization. Francis was saddened because he feared power and wealth as much as most men fear hunger and cold. He believed that men should follow the example of Christ and live without rich food and fine clothing. Only in this way, he believed, could Christ's church truly follow him.

In the fall of 1226, Francis became very sick and suffered from an eye disease. Although he was sick, he did not lose his happy heart. He was a servant of Christ in God's wonderful world. He put his love of nature and his joy at serving God in this fine hymn:

O most high, almighty, good Lord God, to thee belong praise, glory, honor, and all blessing!

Praised be my Lord God with all his creatures, and specially our brother the sun, who brings us the day and who brings us the light; fair is he and shines with a very great splendor; O Lord, he signifies to us thee!

Praised be my Lord for our sister the moon, and for the stars, the which he has set clear and lovely in Heaven.

Praised be my Lord for our brother the wind, and for air and cloud, calms and all weather by the which thou upholdest life in all creatures.

Praised be my Lord for our sister water, who is very serviceable unto us and humble and precious and clean.

Praised be my Lord for our brother fire, through whom thou givest us light in the darkness; and he is bright and pleasant and very mighty and strong.

Praised be my Lord for our mother the earth, the which doth sustain us and keep us, and bringeth forth divers fruits and flowers of many colors, and grass.

Praised be my Lord for all those who pardon one another for his love's sake, and who endure weakness and tribulation; blessed are they who peaceably shall endure, for thou, O most Highest, shalt give them a crown.

When Francis knew that he had not much longer to live, he added another stanza welcoming his sister Death:

Praised be my Lord for our sister, the death of the body, from which no man escapeth. Woe to him who dieth in mortal sin! Blessed are they who are found walking by thy most holy will, for the second death shall have no power to do them harm.

Praise ye and bless the Lord, and give thanks unto him and serve him with great humility.

6. Martin Luther

HERE I STAND

PART ONE

MARTIN LUTHER WAS nine years old when Christopher Columbus sailed westward and discovered America. When Luther was twenty-six, Magellan began his famous voyage around the world. By this time the first printing presses had been at work for more than sixty years. News of new discoveries and new ideas spread rapidly because books could be printed instead of being written by hand. It was an exciting time to live.

Although the world was changing rapidly, the church had remained almost unchanged for hundreds of years. Bibles were still very expensive. Only wealthy bishops or noblemen owned their own copies. Churches and libraries often kept their Bibles chained to high stands. Very few people ever read the Bible for themselves.

In 1483 a baby was born in Germany who was to renew and reform the life of the church when he grew to manhood. He would do this by teaching that the Bible is the best guide for a Christian.

Childhood and Latin School

The little cottage in the village of Eisleben was quiet now. Darkness was settling over the village. The newborn baby was sleeping. His mother was tired, too, but she was proud of her new son. She and her husband Hans whispered together about their new child.

"He should be baptized tomorrow," Hans said. "Since tomorrow is Saint Martin's Day, let's call him Martin."

So it was that on November 11, 1483, the son of a German miner was baptized in the village of Eisleben, Germany, and given the name Martin Luther.

Martin's parents were thrifty, hard-working people. His father worked in the copper mines nearby. Hans Luther was very strict with his son. He wanted Martin to learn the difference between right and wrong early in life.

As Martin grew older, Hans Luther discovered that his young son was no ordinary child. He could learn very quickly and easily. He could memorize whole pages just by reading them over a few times. Hans Luther did not want his son to waste his unusual talents, so he decided to send him to a special school.

During the fifteenth century, Latin was the language used by educated people throughout Europe. Books were printed in Latin. Classes were taught in Latin. Anyone who wanted to get an education had to learn Latin in addition to his own language. So Martin first went to "Latin school."

At Latin school Martin worked hard. Like the other students, he had only a tiny room to sleep in. For his food he went begging from house to house with a band of singing students.

In 1501 Martin was ready to enter the university. "You must study law," his father said. Hans Luther wanted his son to become an important government official.

At the University

What a jolly student Luther was! He liked to play his lute and sing gay student songs with his friends. His classmates called him a musician and a philosopher because he was interested in everything that went on in the world around him. Luther also liked to think seriously about the meaning of things.

Deep within himself, Luther had a question which he often asked himself. "When God calls me before his judgment throne, he will see that I am a sinner," he thought. "Then God will surely punish me. What can I do to win God's *love?*"

Sometimes Luther would wake up in a cold sweat in the middle of the night thinking about God's punishment. He could not seem to find an answer to the question in his heart.

As a student Luther often went to the university library. One day he saw a huge, thick book chained to a high stand in the library. It was a Latin Bible! Luther had seen a whole Bible only once or twice before. He opened the big book and began to read the page where the book had fallen open. He read the Old Testament story of a woman named Hannah who went to the temple to pray when she was troubled. "She prayed to the Lord, and wept bitterly," Luther read.

Luther began to think about himself. "I have prayed earnestly as Hannah did," he whispered. He read on eagerly to find out what happened to Hannah. Soon a bell rang to mark the beginning of the next class. Luther had to close the book and go to class. But he promised himself that he would come back to read more.

As he ran to class, Luther thought about the story of
Hannah he had read in the First Book of Samuel. It was
new and strange to him. Martin knew many stories from
the Gospels which he had heard read in church. Now he
wanted to own a Bible and read it for himself—all of it.

In his little room Luther continued to read and study
his thick, heavy law books. He memorized page after page
of laws, but he was unhappy with his studies. He did not
want to be a lawyer. "I can learn all the laws in the world,"
he thought, "but they will never help me answer the most
important question of all."

Bolt of Lightning

In July, 1505, Luther left home after his vacation and
began hiking back to the university. As he walked through
the dark German forest, thick, black thunder clouds
gathered above. Thunder crashed around him. The whole
forest echoed with the sounds of the storm. Suddenly a
bolt of lightning struck near Luther and knocked him to
the ground. Luther was terrified. If God called him to the
judgment throne now, he would surely condemn him as a
sinner. What could he do? In a loud voice he prayed:
"Help me, Saint Anne! I will become a monk!"

"If God spares me," Luther thought, "I must learn to
live a holy life that will please him. Surely I can learn to
follow God's ways in a monastery."

Luther reached the university safely. For two weeks he
pondered the great decision he had made in the forest.
Then he sold his books—all except two books of Latin
poems that he loved. On the night of July 16, he gave a
farewell party for his student friends at the university. The

next morning the students brought him to the door of the monastery of the Augustinian monks. The door opened, and Luther walked into another world.

The monastery was a large, quiet building. Each monk lived in a tiny, unheated room and slept on a narrow bed made of boards. After a trial period of about a year, Luther took the vows of a monk. He promised never to marry, never to own anything, and to obey the head of the monastery without question.

Luther lived the strict life of a monk. He ate the plain food of the monastery without complaining. Often he fasted. At certain hours of the day and night he prayed with the other monks. He spent his time praying and studying, helping in the kitchen, and begging for the monastery. In 1507 his studies were completed and Luther became a priest.

Professor at Wittenberg

The head of the monastery to which Luther belonged was a man named John Staupitz. He became very fond of Luther, for he recognized that this young monk was an unusually talented man. In 1508 he sent Luther to Wittenberg to study further and prepare to become a professor. As a present, he gave the young monk a Latin Bible bound in red leather to take with him. Luther studied the Bible until he knew large parts of it by heart.

But the question in Luther's heart was still unanswered. The more Luther studied the Bible, the more he came to understand how sinful he was. Often he would go to an older, more experienced monk to confess his sins. Sometimes he spent hours listing all his sinful thoughts and

deeds. As soon as he had finished his confession, he would think of other sins he had forgotten to name. Luther despaired of ever winning forgiveness for all his sins.

When Luther had finished his studies at Wittenberg, John Staupitz and Frederick the Wise, the ruler of Saxony, saw to it that the young monk became professor of the Bible at the small University of Wittenberg. Now Luther not only had to study the Bible for himself, but he also had to explain it to his students.

One day as Luther was preparing a lecture, he stopped to read again the first chapter of Romans:

For I am not ashamed of the gospel; it is the power of God for salvation to every one who has faith . . . (Romans 1:16).

Luther had read this chapter dozens of times before. But now it seemed as if the doors of heaven opened to him. "God does love me," he said to himself. "God does forgive me. I can come before God's throne of judgment because God *makes* me righteous in *faith*. I do not need to be afraid of God."

Tears of joy ran down Luther's face. Only a person who had fought long and hard against the sins in his own mind and heart can understand how he felt. Luther was no longer afraid of God. A great love flooded his heart.

Luther now had something special to teach his students. His lectures became more exciting than ever before. Students crowded into the university lecture halls to hear him. As they listened, they began to understand that nothing a person *does* can make God love him. God already loves sinful men. He cared enough about us to send his own Son to save us. If we *trust* in God, he will help and save us. Luther opened the way for a new understanding of the Bible.

Corruption in the Church

The more Luther learned to understand what God is like, the more unhappy he became with what the church was like. Luther taught his students that the Bible is the best guide for a Christian. But when he saw what the church was doing, he saw how far away from the Bible the church had turned.

For example, the church taught that people could easily get forgiveness of sins. All they had to do was come to church and touch or look at the relic of a saint. The relic might be one of the saint's bones or a piece of clothing the saint had worn. The people were told that the saints had done so many good works that there was a special treasury in heaven of extra good deeds. A saint could ask God to use one of his extra good deeds to pay for the sins of someone still on earth. If a person touched the leg bone of a saint and prayed to the saint, the saint might ask God to use some of his extra good deeds to forgive that person's sins.

Wittenberg was a good place to go to see relics. Frederick the Wise, the ruler of Saxony, had collected 5,005 different relics and put them in the big Castle Church. People came from miles around to see and touch them.

Worse than that, a monk named John Tetzel was traveling in neighboring lands to sell letters of forgiveness. These letters were called "indulgences" and were given out by the pope. For example, a grandmother might take her savings out of an old sock and buy an indulgence. John Tetzel would tell her that the letter guaranteed a certain amount of forgiveness of sins for her dead husband.

The reason Tetzel was selling the indulgences was to collect money to build a great new church—St. Peter's in Rome. Tetzel promised everyone that an indulgence would reduce the number of years a person would have to spend in purgatory. The Roman Catholic church taught that after a person dies he must go to purgatory and suffer for his sins until he becomes pure enough to go to heaven.

No wonder people crowded around Tetzel. They wanted to buy off God from punishing them so many years

in purgatory. They thought it a good bargain to be able to buy a letter that would pay for a hundred years less in purgatory! By doing a good deed for the church, they thought they could earn less punishment in purgatory.

Luther saw more and more clearly how dangerous it was for people to buy indulgences, touch the relics, and worship the saints. Then they would never get to know God's love and forgiveness. They would never know what true repentance means. They would never realize how sinful they were if they thought they could buy God's forgiveness with money. This was not only wrong, it was also terribly dangerous for the souls of the people. All summer long Luther worried about this problem.

The Ninety-Five Theses

Luther looked at his calendar. Soon it would be November 1, 1517—that was All Saints' Day. On that day people would come from far and wide to the Castle Church of Wittenberg to see a special display of relics. This gave Luther an idea. He would strike a blow against the whole business of indulgences and relics.

What he had in mind was a dangerous thing to do. That was why he kept it secret. No one else should be endangered but himself.

Luther's plan was to start a debate among the professors about indulgences. In such a debate, everyone would have to study the Bible to find out what it said. They would find out how wrong and dangerous indulgences were. Then the bishops and the pope would have to listen. Surely then they would abolish indulgences.

To begin the debate, Luther wrote a list of ninety-five arguments or "theses" to challenge any scholar to debate with him. He wrote in Latin, the language of educated men. On October 31, the day before All Saints' Day, he nailed a printed copy to the door of the church. Everyone would see the Ninety-Five Theses when they came to church the next day.

Luther's plan was a good one, but it failed. Not a single professor took up the challenge to debate with Luther. Instead, someone translated the Ninety-Five Theses into Ger-

man and had them printed as a booklet. Soon people all over Germany were reading Luther's arguments and talking about them with great excitement. It was time, many said, to *reform* the church and rid it of false teaching.

PART TWO

WHEN EVERYONE began to talk about Luther's theses, the big question was, "Will the pope listen to these arguments from the Bible?"

Would the bishops reform the church to which almost everybody in Europe belonged? Or would they arrest Luther as a heretic and burn him at the stake?

The bishops and the pope read Luther's plain, bold statements. They decided that Luther was indeed a heretic and that he must be destroyed. On June 15, 1520, the pope sent a message to the new emperor, Charles V. The message condemned Luther and all his writings.

Charles V came to Germany in the fall of 1520 and summoned all the princes and bishops of Germany to an assembly in the city of Worms. This assembly was called a diet. The emperor declared that the diet must condemn Luther as a heretic. Then he ordered Luther to come to Worms and promised him safety for a trip from Wittenberg to Worms and back again.

Witness Before the Emperor

Tuesday after Easter, 1521, Martin Luther climbed into a wagon provided by the town council of Wittenberg and started on his trip to Worms. Luther's friends advised him to stay home because they did not trust the emperor. But Luther said he would go, even if there were as many devils in Worms as tiles on the roofs. At Worms, Luther thought he could speak face to face with the bishops. He would explain *why* his theses were true because they agreed with God's Word. He would take the Bible and explain it to the emperor and the bishops.

The diet did not want to listen to any explanations. The day after Luther arrived he was led into the great hall where all the princes and bishops were gathered. The big, burly court official took charge. "All you have to do," he said, "is answer two questions."

He pointed to a pile of more than twenty books which Luther had written. "First, are you willing to confess that you have written these books? Second, are you ready to renounce these books?"

Of course, Luther was ready to say that the books were his. But since the second question was so important, he asked for time to think it over so that he might give a proper answer.

The next day Luther came before the diet again. He stood up to speak and before the official in charge could stop him, he said that not all his books were the same. Some were books of prayers. Others were written against the enemies of the gospel. Luther said he realized that he was human and could make mistakes. Perhaps he had criticized other men too sharply. If so, he was ready to apologize. If the emperor or the bishops or anyone could show him that any of his books were wrong and did not agree with the Bible, he would be the first to throw the book into the fire.

The court official was impatient. "Give us a short, clear answer," he demanded.

Then Luther said: "Since Your Majesty and Your Lordships ask for a simple reply, I will give you one without horns or teeth. Unless I am proved to be wrong by the testimony of Scriptures and by plain reasoning . . . I am bound in conscience and hold fast to the Word of God. I cannot and I will not retract anything, for it is neither safe nor right to act against one's conscience. God help me! Amen."

What a stir this made! Here stood one man against the bishops, the emperor, the pope. Against him stood all the power of the church and the empire. He had no other weapon than the Word of God. Here stood Luther!

Many in the crowded room hissed, "A heretic! A heretic!" The emperor's Spanish guards shouted, "Take him to the fire!"

At any other time Luther might well have been burned as a heretic. But now the diet had other extremely important business. The emperor needed soldiers and money for the war with France which seemed to be coming. He especially needed the help of Luther's ruler and friend, Frederick the Wise. He dared not make enemies of the German princes by putting Luther to death. So the emperor kept his promise and let Luther leave Worms safely. Everyone knew that the emperor's promise was good only as far as Wittenberg.

From now on, the diet declared, Luther was "outside the law." Anyone who killed him would not be punished. No one was to give him food or shelter, for he was a heretic.

Kidnapped in the Forest

As Luther's wagon rattled peacefully through the woods toward Wittenberg, a band of four or five horsemen suddenly surrounded it. The strange horsemen stopped the wagon and demanded to know who was in the wagon. When they heard the name Martin Luther, they dragged Luther from the wagon and rode off into the woods with him. As soon as they were out of sight, they apologized for seeming to be so rough. Late that night they brought Luther to Wartburg Castle.

For the next several months almost no one in Germany knew where Luther was. Only a few friends knew that he was safely hidden in a castle in the forest hills of Germany.

Luther lived in a secret room in Wartburg Castle. He dressed like a noble and grew a beard. People in the castle called him "Squire George" and sometimes he rode out of the castle to go hunting with the nobles.

In Wartburg Castle Luther kept busy. He worked day and night to translate the New Testament into German. He waited eagerly for news from Wittenberg. Reports were sent to Luther about riots in the churches when the priests put on everyday clothes.

Finally Luther could no longer stand it to stay in hiding. He went back to Wittenberg and, when he appeared in the pulpit of the Castle Church, a great crowd came to hear him. Luther helped turn the Roman Catholic churches in Wittenberg into "evangelical" churches. Evangelical means "according to the gospel." He went back to the university and lectured on the Bible.

How long would Luther be safe? He did not know. Luther fully expected to be captured and put to death as a heretic. He was not afraid, and worked as hard as he could to explain what the Bible teaches about Jesus Christ and man's salvation.

PART THREE

LUTHER QUICKLY became a hero throughout Germany. Wise and learned men, carpenters and bricklayers, housewives and students all read and talked about his teachings. Printers could not publish his books fast enough because so many people wanted to read them. Wherever Luther's books went, his ideas of reforming the church spread.

Students came to Wittenberg from Finland and Scotland, from Holland and England, from Sweden and all parts of Germany to study under Luther. When they returned home, they helped reform the churches in their own lands.

Witness in Time of Trouble and Danger

Life was not easy for Luther. All over Europe people were taking sides, either for him or against him. Luther's enemies spread false stories about him and published cartoons against him. Luther wrote books and pamphlets to defend himself. People in other parts of Europe began setting up evangelical churches in their own lands. Often they asked Luther's advice and help. Then a plague swept through Wittenberg. Many people fled from the city. Luther stayed to help care for the sick and dying. In 1524 and 1525 thousands of German peasants revolted against their rulers and spread fire and destruction through the land. Several times the Turkish armies threatened to march into Europe. Many people were also afraid that the emperor and the pope would soon raise an army to destroy those who followed the teachings of Luther.

In these dangerous times, Luther married Katharine von Bora. The ruler of Saxony gave them the big, empty monas-

tery building to use as a home. Luther's wife swept out the cobwebs. She planted a big garden. Soon the Luther home became a busy household. Many people lived with Luther and his family. Some were poor students who came for food and lodging. Others were orphaned relatives. There were always several guests. Every day students and guests gathered at Luther's dinner table. There they discussed many things, some serious, some not so serious. Some of the students made notes of things Luther said. These notes have been gathered in a book called *Luther's Table Talk*.

Luther preached often in the Castle Church, not only on Sundays but also on certain weekdays. With the help of other professors he finished translating the Bible into German. He wrote a catechism for parents to use in their homes so that everyone could learn the most important things about the Christian faith.

He helped his friend Melanchthon write a statement of what he and his followers believed and taught. This statement is called the *Augsburg Confession*. It was signed by many princes in Germany and handed to the emperor. Lutheran churches throughout the world still accept this confession today.

Luther did not give up his music. He liked to play his lute and sing with his family. He wrote hymns and these were gathered in the first Lutheran hymnbook. It was said that Luther's great hymns sang the Reformation into the hearts of the people.

Luther's Last Witness

In the icy winter of 1546 Luther traveled to Eisleben, the town where he was born. He was called to help settle a quarrel in a noble family. Luther was successful, but in the night of February 17 he became deathly sick. His sons and his friends came into the room. They heard Luther's last prayer:

> O my heavenly Father, God and Father of our Lord Jesus Christ, Thou God of all comfort, I thank Thee, that Thou hast revealed to me Thy dear Son, Jesus Christ, in whom I believe, whom I have preached and confessed, and whom I have loved and praised. I pray Thee, dear Lord Jesus Christ, that my soul may be committed to Thee. O heavenly Father, though I must leave this body and this life, I know for certain that I will be with Thee for eternity and that no one can tear me out of Thy hands.

Shortly after midnight Luther died in his sleep. But his strong faith and his witness in his books and his songs live on in the great church that bears his name.

7. William Tyndale

THE BIBLE FOR THE PEOPLE

SLOWLY A SHIP with square sails moved into the London harbor. It was loaded down with sacks of grain. Those were the days when King Henry VIII ruled England and when Martin Luther taught at Wittenberg University.

Jeffrey tapped his feet impatiently on the dock as he watched the slow ship. He took a quick look around to see if anyone was watching. Then he felt his shirt to be sure the letter was safe in his pocket.

"Above all, keep it secret," Simon, the grain merchant, had warned Jeffrey.

There! The ship was tied up at last. Jeffrey leaped aboard and ran to find the captain. He handed him the letter. The captain read it and looked Jeffrey over carefully. Then he said, "Come to my cabin."

When they were alone in the cabin, the captain said, "All right! Now listen carefully. Some of the sacks of wheat have a special mark. Those are the ones for Simon Fyshe, the grain merchant. You have a cart? Good!"

Jeffrey worked fast. Soon his cart rumbled through the narrow streets of London toward the shop of his friend, Simon Fyshe. Within an hour, Jeffrey and the old grain merchant began to rip the sacks open.

"Careful, not so fast," said Simon. "Don't forget that wheat is valuable, too. Especially now when crops have failed people will be glad to buy our wheat."

Smuggled Bibles

"True," Jeffrey replied. "But what they want even more is this!" Out from under the wheat he pulled a dusty book and held it high. "The Word of God in English!"

He handed the book to Simon and reached into the sack for more.

It was exciting to open the book and read the Gospels in plain English words. "Master Tyndale makes the words speak clear, doesn't he!" exclaimed the grain merchant.

"I've heard that Tyndale once told a priest who didn't know his Bible, 'If God spare my life, before many years I will cause the boy who drives the plow to know more of the Scripture than you do,'" said Jeffrey.

"Even a plowboy can read and understand this," Simon Fyshe agreed.

Fyshe had many visitors in the next few days. Hidden in the bundles they carried away were the precious books. A Mr. Bradford took a package to a monk near Reading. Other bundles went to Cambridge University.

The Bishop of London tried to stop the flow of smuggled Bibles. He forbade any unauthorized translation of the Bible into English. The Bishop of London bought as many copies of Tyndale's English Bible as he could and burned them at Paul's Cross in London. Anyone who owned an English Bible was fined or put in prison. Some persons were even burned as heretics. The harder the bishop worked, the more Bibles appeared. They came in the baggage of travelers. They came buried in sacks of wheat or packed in bales of wool.

Where did they come from? Who was this William Tyndale who was translating the Bible?

Spies were sent to Europe to find Tyndale. "He is everywhere and nowhere," wrote one of the spies. Tyndale was called a heretic because he translated the Bible into common English without the permission of the bishop. His life would be in danger if his enemies could find him.

Tyndale's Secret Work

William Tyndale was a learned man who had been a priest in England. His mind was fixed on one idea, to translate God's holy Word from Greek and Hebrew manuscripts into English so that everyone could read it. He asked the Bishop of London for permission to make an English translation, but he was turned away. The king and the leaders of the church agreed that the Bible must be in Latin. No one was to be allowed to make an English translation.

Then Tyndale disappeared. No one in England knew where he went. Just about this time a mysterious Englishman signed up as a student at Wittenberg University. The name he wrote in the university book was *William Daltin*. Perhaps this was a secret way of writing "Tindal." (Daltin. Tin-dal.)

If this really was Tyndale, we can be sure that he learned much from Martin Luther about translating the Bible. Tyndale set to work to make his dream of an English Bible come true. Soon he moved to Cologne to be near the printer of his secret English book. As quickly as he finished part of the translation, he gave the pages to the printers to set in type.

One day a man named Dobneck came to the printers in Cologne. He wanted them to print some of his books against Luther and got to know the printers quite well.

Often Dobneck stayed in the shop to talk with them, and once after they had had several cups of wine, he heard a printer boast that whether King Henry of England liked it or not, in a short time England would be Lutheran. Dobneck listened to the drunken printer talk about two Englishmen who were hiding in the city and who were skilled in many languages.

Dobneck made up his mind to find the secret translator. He invited several of the printers to his room and brought out more and more wine to drink. Loose-tongued from drinking, one man stayed behind and told Dobneck a secret. In the shop they were printing three thousand copies of the New Testament in English. English merchants were paying for the books, and the work was partly finished already.

Dobneck moved quickly. He went to the authorities to tell them about the "heretics" and their work. Men were sent to seize the books, but Tyndale was warned just in time. Snatching up the parts of the book already printed, he escaped from Cologne and went to Worms. Worms was a Lutheran city and there he was safe. In Worms he found other printers and finished his translation of the New Testament. Merchants promised to smuggle the copies into England.

Witness at Antwerp

So far Tyndale had been successful. Now he began to work on translating the Old Testament. He decided to go to the harbor town of Antwerp, just across from England. There he could keep in touch with travelers from his homeland. Tyndale knew that Antwerp was a dangerous place because it was ruled by Roman Catholics. But he felt safe as long as he lived in the house of the English merchants. Thomas Poyntz, a food merchant, worked eagerly for the Reformation. He gave Tyndale a room where he could work in secret.

Two days a week Tyndale set apart for his "pastime." On Mondays he went about the city to help and encourage refugees from England who had fled to Antwerp to escape religious persecution. On Saturdays he walked about Antwerp "seeking every corner and hole where he suspected any poor person to dwell." He tried to help these poor people in any way he could.

"Be careful of strangers," Thomas Poyntz, the merchant, warned Tyndale. "I don't trust that new Englishman, Henry Phillips."

Tyndale did not heed the warning. He rather liked the young man and they were often together. One day Phillips made sure that the merchant, Poyntz, was away. He invited Tyndale to have dinner with him. As they came down the steps out of the house, two men were standing in the street. Phillips pointed down at Tyndale's head and the two men seized and bound Tyndale and dragged him to the prison of Vilvorde near Brussels.

Tyndale was kept in prison for more than four months. The jailer and his daughter became Protestants because of Tyndale's influence. In a letter from prison to the governor Tyndale wrote:

> And I ask to be allowed to have a lamp in the evening; it is indeed wearisome sitting alone in the dark. But most of all I beg and beseech your clemency to be urgent with the commissary, that he will kindly permit me to have the Hebrew Bible, Hebrew grammar, and Hebrew dictionary, that I may pass the time in that study. In return you may obtain what you most desire, so only that it be for the salvation of your soul. But if any other decision has been taken concerning me, to be carried out before winter, I will be patient, abiding the will of God, to the glory of the grace of my Lord Jesus Christ; whose Spirit, I pray, may ever direct your heart. Amen.

Early in October 1536 Tyndale was burned at the stake as a heretic. His last thoughts were for his country and his Bible translation, for he prayed, "Lord, open the King of England's eyes."

8. John Wesley

GOD'S MESSENGER ON HORSEBACK

IT WAS A WARM, bright day in October, 1735. John and Charles Wesley boarded the ship waiting in England. They were going to North America! John was to serve as a missionary pastor to the Indians. Charles was to be secretary to an important official in the colony of Georgia. As the two brothers crossed the narrow deck, John's thoughts raced back to his days at Oxford University.

How he would miss studying and worshiping with his friends! Other students had laughed at him and his friends and had called them the "Holy Club" because they tried to live as Christians. "We must continue to set aside special times each day for prayer and study," John thought.

John Wesley lived in a time when it was no longer dangerous to be a Protestant. Almost everyone in England belonged to the Church of England, which had broken away from the Roman Catholic church. But no one seemed to get very excited about their faith. Services were held in church every Sunday, but they often seemed coldly formal. The church was not very interested in helping the poor or seeking out those who did not come to church. At the university, the "Holy Club" had tried to help the sick and the poor, visiting them at certain times every week. They did something new: they visited people in the terrible jails of that time. Other students merely laughed at them. "They're so methodical about their religion," they jeered. "They're nothing but 'method-ists.'"

During the long four-month voyage to Georgia, the Wesleys made friends among the passengers on the tiny ship. Among them were Christians from Germany called the Moravians. The two English brothers admired these men and women for their warm, eager, confident faith in Jesus Christ. Even during the winter storms that battered the ship, the Moravians prayed cheerfully and confidently. Their witness made a deep impression on John Wesley.

When the Wesley brothers reached Georgia, John learned that he had been appointed pastor of the colony. He was to work among the settlers, not among the Indians. But the settlers had little time for the rather formal English clergyman. They were busy with their own quarrels and gossip. What was worse, John Wesley began to feel that something was lacking in his Christian faith. He did not feel within himself the warm love of God as the Moravians did. And he could not preach about a love that he did not feel. His trip to America was a failure. Deeply discouraged, John Wesley decided to return to England.

A Changed Person

One evening in May 1738, shortly after he had returned to England, John Wesley attended a meeting at Aldersgate

Street in London. During the meeting someone read from the writings of Martin Luther. As he listened Wesley felt a strange and wonderful peace come over him. That night he wrote in his diary, "I felt my heart strangely warmed." Now Wesley felt sure that God had indeed forgiven *his* sins. Now he knew that he believed with all his heart. With tremendous enthusiasm Wesley began to tell others about his new faith in Jesus Christ.

Wesley preached with such earnestness now that "respectable" people began to wonder about him. Wesley was trying to bring people close to a Christ who had come to *change* people's lives, to deliver them from their sins. Most respectable people did not want to be changed by their faith. They thought it scandalous that a preacher excite people with his message. Pastors even refused to allow Wesley to preach in their churches. At his home church in Epworth, where Wesley's father had been pastor for many years, Wesley was not allowed to speak from the pulpit. So he went to his father's grave and preached there.

Crowds flowed to hear Wesley preach. Most of the people that came were men and women who worked in mines and factories and did not usually go to church. The church had never shown any real interest or concern for these working people. They were hungry to hear about the Christ who had come to save them from their sins. They longed to hear how God can change a man or woman.

Instead of settling down as a pastor in a stone church building somewhere in England, Wesley rode on horseback up and down the countryside of England, Scotland, Wales, and Ireland. Wherever he went he preached to all who would listen, often as early as five a.m.

As he traveled about, Wesley did not establish new churches. He did not want to leave the Church of England. Instead he started small groups called societies. These societies met to study the Bible and to worship and pray. And they tried to live their new faith by helping others.

Witness Before Mobs

When Wesley rode into town, he was often met by an angry mob instead of a welcoming crowd. Respectable and not-so-respectable people whispered, "Wesley is a dangerous man. He might start a revolution!" It took courage to join Wesley's societies, for the mobs often beat the members of the societies. Sometimes they burned and tore down the homes of the "methodists." People even lost their jobs if they became "methodists."

Once in 1743 a mob gathered in front of the house where Wesley was staying in Cornwall, in the southwestern part of England. "Bring out the Canorum!" the mob roared.

Inside John Wesley was working busily at a desk. As the mob outside shouted, he wrote in his secret diary, "Canorum—a word which the Cornish people generally use instead of Methodist."

"They're out in the hall now," Kitty warned. She was the only other person in the house. Everyone else had fled.

Wesley got up from the desk and walked toward the thin partition that was the only barrier to the mob. There was a burst of yells from the hall outside.

"Oh, sir, what must we do?" wailed poor Kitty.

"We must pray," Wesley answered quietly.

"But sir," she sobbed, "wouldn't it be better to hide?"

"It is best for me to stay here," Wesley answered.

"There are sailors in the mob," Kitty pleaded. "Their ships just docked in the harbor. They'll be the worst."

Just then there was a cry from the hallway, louder than the confused roar of the mob. "On, lads! On!"

There was a brief pause—then a rush of heavy shoulders against the thin partition. Away went the hinges. The door fell into the room. The mob poured in. Wesley calmly stepped forward into the middle of the rough men.

"Here I am," he said. "Do any of you have anything to say to me? To which of you have I done any wrong?"

Kitty watched as John Wesley spoke first to one man, then to another. His words seemed to work like magic. The men began to listen to what Wesley had to say and forgot their other plans. They stood quietly looking at his face and making no move to hurt him.

Wesley followed the men out into the street. "Neighbors! Countrymen!" he raised his voice so that many could hear him. "Do you all want to hear me speak?"

"Yes! Yes!" came shouts. "Let him speak. Let him speak. No one shall stop him!" the crowd shouted.

Wesley had no platform to stand on. He was dwarfed by the broad-shouldered sailors and working men who crowded around him. Nevertheless, he began to speak in a quiet, but firm voice. "God loves you," he began. "He sent his own Son to save you from your sins."

Gradually those closest to Wesley began to quiet down and listen. Others at the edge of the mob pushed in to get at the preacher. Two of the men who had been among those who broke into the house turned on the crowd, "No one touches Mr. Wesley!"

What Christ Can Do

Mobs often gathered to threaten John Wesley. More often, however, hundreds gathered to hear the preacher who dared to preach in open fields and meadows. They grew quiet as the tiny man with burning eyes spoke about the Christ who had come to save men from their sins.

And what a change Wesley's preaching made! In towns where there had often been fighting and drunkenness, people became sober and peaceful Christians. They tried to show the change Christ had made in their lives through their actions. Wesley often said, "This is not my work. This is what Jesus Christ can do in a man's heart."

John Wesley became known as the preacher on horseback. Through rain and snow, heat and cold he rode from place to place, often reading as he went. In the fifty-two years that Wesley traveled, he rode more than 225,000 miles and preached some 40,000 sermons.

After Wesley's death the people who had joined his societies left the Church of England and formed a new church. It became known as the Methodist church. Through this church, Wesley's witness to Christ has spread far and wide through England and North America.

PART III

New Ways to Witness

9. Johann Sebastian Bach

TO THE GLORY OF GOD

SEBASTIAN COULD NOT SLEEP. The moonlight streaming through his window kept him awake—awake to think of the music he wanted. Downstairs, in a locked cupboard in his brother's library, lay a thin book with the music of the great German composers. How Sebastian longed to see that music; how his fingers yearned to play it! But his brother had forbidden him the book.

"You are too young," he had said sternly. "That is no music for a ten-year-old. Wait until you are older."

But Sebastian was tired of the beginner's exercises he had to practice. If only he could see that music . . .

Quietly he slipped out of bed. Cautiously he crept downstairs to the cupboard where the music was kept. He peered through the lattice door that kept him from the book he so much wanted. He hesitated, listening to the small sounds of the cold and sleeping house. Then, sliding cautious, exploring fingers through the lattice work, he touched the corner of the book. If he could roll it until it was thin enough to slip through the opening—there, he had it! He had the precious book!

Now that he actually held the book in his hands, Sebastian trembled with excitement. He carried his treasure to the table and began, slowly and carefully, to copy parts of the music. He forgot how cold he was. Even the fear of being caught melted away. Nothing mattered but the music. Only when the moon went down and it was too dark to see did he roll up the book, slip it back into the cupboard, and go yawning—and happy—to bed.

The next six months were exciting ones for Sebastian. Every day he practiced the simple music his brother gave him; but every moonlit night he bent his head close to the music he loved, studying each measure, humming it softly as he copied, imagining how it would sound when he played it. And then one terrible night his brother caught him at the forbidden work and angrily snatched the book and what he had copied away from him. But it was too late: he could not take away the music that had sung its way into Sebastian's heart and head. Sebastian had lost his careful copy; he had permanently damaged his eyes working in the dim light. But he could play the music he so much admired!

Master at the Organ

The town of Eisenach, where Johann Sebastian Bach was born in 1685, is in central Germany. In the nearby forests Boniface had brought the gospel to pagan tribes a thousand years before. This was the part of Germany in which Martin Luther had grown up. And here the name of Bach had been famous for music for nearly two hundred years

—so famous that in this part of the country every musician
was called a "Bach"!

All the Bach family loved music. Most of them made
their living as musicians or teachers of music. And when
the whole family got together, there were enough good
singers and players for a concert. What fun they had singing and playing their own compositions, making songs
that were laughing and gay, and music deep and beautiful
as that of the great cathedrals. But none of them loved music more than did Sebastian. While Sebastian was still very
small, his father taught him to sing and play the violin.

When Sebastian was nine years old, his parents died,
and he and his younger brother went to live with their married brother in Ohrdruf. During the next five years Sebastian learned to play the organ and clavier, sang in the
church choir, and learned much about music. Sebastian
knew how hard it was for his brother to provide for his
own family along with his brothers. And so when he heard
that there were singing jobs at the famous choir school of
St. Michael's in distant Lüneberg, Sebastian and a friend
decided to walk the two hundred miles to the town.

For three years Sebastian stayed at St. Michael's school,
singing in the choir and playing the clavier and violin in ex-
change for his education. He studied music, church his-
tory, the teachings of the Lutheran church, as well as
other subjects; but his happiest hours were spent at the organ. No books were locked away from him now. He was
free to practice the music of the great masters and to try
out new melodies and arrangements of his own. Sometimes he would walk to cities far away to hear great or-
ganists play.

Before long, Sebastian's own fame as a musician began
to spread. When the town of Arnstadt needed a church
organist, they asked him to come. He worked at his music
until he became the finest organist anywhere. It is said
that once he visited a tiny village church and played so
magnificently on their poor organ that someone who did
not know who was playing exclaimed: "This can only be
an angel from heaven—or Bach himself!"

Another time Bach was visiting the city of Dresden. At
that time there was another famous guest in the city, Marchand, the organist at the royal court of France. The
Frenchman had never heard of this German organist and
was amused when someone suggested that the two have a
contest of their playing. What? Match the great French
royal organist with this unknown? It was really funny! But
at last he agreed. The contest was set for the following
evening. Meanwhile Marchand secretly had a chance to
hear Bach play. When the time for the contest came, Bach
arrived promptly. The company waited and waited for
Marchand. Finally someone was sent to his inn to see why
he had not come. The messenger returned with the news
that Marchand had left and taken all his luggage with
him. Apparently he was afraid to have his playing com-
pared with that of the man he had laughed at.

To God Alone Be Glory

Many princes wanted Bach as a court musician. For
several years Bach served as organist and concertmaster
for some of the German princes. But most of his life he
spent playing and writing music for the church. In 1723 he
became organist and choir director at St. Thomas' Church

in Leipzig. The job paid only a fourth as much as his po-
sition at the court of the prince; he had to conduct the
choirs of four churches and spend much of his time teaching music, Latin, and Luther's catechism to the boys of St.
Thomas' School, who were not always interested or willing
to learn.

It was hard for many people to understand why he
should be willing to do this. But Bach knew he had made
the right choice. He believed that all musical talent was a
gift from God and that it should be treasured and used in
God's service. He believed that writing and performing
music are really worship, and that every note should be
good enough to dedicate to God.

Sunday after Sunday Bach poured his love for God into
music. During the twenty-seven years he spent at Leipzig
he wrote nearly three hundred cantatas, each one telling a
Bible story or singing out the meaning of a Bible passage.
He set to music his favorite verses from the psalms, the
prophets, and the New Testament. Many of his works tell
in music the story of Jesus' life and death and resurrection.
He even set to music part of the Nicene Creed.

> I acknowledge one baptism for the remission of sins, and I
> look for the resurrection of the dead and the life of the
> world to come.

He took old hymn tunes and words and gave them new
and richer musical settings. No one has ever set the Lutheran faith to music better than Bach did.

And at the top of every piece of his music, even on the
simple exercises he wrote for his own children, Bach
marked the letters J.J. They stood for the Latin words
Jesu Juva, which in English mean "Jesus, help me." At the

end of his work he often scribbled the letters S.D.G.—
Soli Deo Gloria—which mean "to God alone the glory."

The years at Leipzig were busy years for Bach. The music that rushed to his mind and filled his heart to praise
God could be sung and played in church services where it
helped others in their worship of God. His happiness did
not come from being famous. The world of his time hon-
ored him as a fine organist, but many people did not understand or like the music he wrote. They would not have
believed then that the time would come when musicians
would consider him the greatest composer who ever lived.

The music Bach wrote was stored away carelessly in
the cupboards of the choir school; sometimes pages of it
were even used to wrap up a schoolboy's lunch! One of his
greatest works, *The St. Matthew Passion,* was performed
only once during his lifetime, on Good Friday, 1729. A
hundred years passed before it was sung again!

Bach's happiness came from a life lived very close to
God. He thanked God for the gift of music and used it to
express his love to God and devotion to Jesus Christ, his
Savior.

10. Amalie Sieveking

NOT ALMS BUT A FRIEND

A TALL, DARK-EYED girl, about ten years old, stood by the side of the road, watching. The road was crowded with refugees, all moving in one direction—toward the safety of the city of Hamburg. Some were carrying bundles. Some pushed wooden carts filled with their belongings. There were old grandmothers hobbling along, and thin-faced children.

It was an unhappy procession that hurried on. Behind them in the far distance were the armies of Napoleon, the mighty French general. Behind them lay burned villages and ruined fields. All hoped to find safety and help in the big harbor city of Hamburg.

But the harbor in Hamburg was quiet. French warships allowed no ships to move in or out of the harbor. Shops were closed and factories were idle. The girl, Amalie Sieveking (ah-*mahl*-yeh *see*-veh-king), had heard what grownups in Hamburg were saying: "So many refugees. We cannot take care of them. There is no work for them

here." As Amalie watched the procession stream by, she wondered what the refugees would do when they reached the city.

Amalie lived in a very different world. Her father was a wealthy merchant and a senator. She lived in a comfortable house in Hamburg. She was never hungry. Although her mother was dead, her father provided a protected life for her in the comfortable family home.

Amalie was a rather shy and solemn girl. She knew that she was supposed to grow up to be a fine and proper lady, like all the women in the best families of Hamburg. But it seemed so dull. A girl was supposed to learn to cook, keep house, and sit stiffly in a chair and embroider. Amalie could do nothing well. She took singing lessons, but she had no voice for music. She took cooking lessons, but her cakes were as poor as her music. Often she was sick, and her body was shaken by violent spasms.

As she grew older, Amalie became more and more lonely. For a time a university student was hired to teach her to read French and English. But as Amalie grew to be a young woman she felt as if she were in a prison. She dreamed of doing something useful and worthwhile, but what could a proper young girl do?

When Amalie was fifteen years old, her father died. After a time, Amalie went to live with her aunt, Madame Brunnemann, and helped her take care of her invalid son. Times were hard in Hamburg. More and more people crowded into the city and beggars filled the streets. When there was work, they sweated in grim factories for long hours and poor wages. But Amalie still lived in a world far apart from the ragged people in the streets.

Like most children of good families in Hamburg, Amalie went to confirmation class at the Lutheran church. The pastor began by having each boy or girl read aloud. Some stood silently, staring at the printed page. If they did not know how to read, the pastor dismissed them from the class. On her way home, Amalie saw one of the girls who had been dismissed. She was leaning against a tree and weeping bitterly. Amalie stopped to talk to her. The girl lived on a little farm outside the city. She could not read. Because there were no schools for poor people there was no chance for her to learn how to read.

"If you want to learn to read," Amalie said, "I'll teach you."

The girl looked at her in amazement. "Do you really mean that?" she asked.

"Of course I do," Amalie said. "Just come to my house. Let me tell you where I live."

So Amalie had her first pupil. Later when she was eighteen, she brought a little girl to her room to teach her to knit. Then when the girl's family governess left, Amalie asked if she could teach the family's three little children.

For the rest of her life Amalie Sieveking taught a class of children like these, three times a week from twelve until three o'clock. She made up her own lessons and later wrote books to use in her classes.

Where Can God Use Me?

When Amalie was twenty-three years old, her beloved brother Gustav died. Amalie was very sad because she had loved Gustav very much. To help cheer her, her brother Henry invited her to visit him in England. In England Amalie read and studied and rested. Gradually she came to a very real and personal faith in Jesus. This new and happy faith came slowly, but Amalie knew that this was God's work in her life.

Still, when Amalie returned to Hamburg, she did not know how to make her life useful to others. She filled page after page of her diary with searching, restless thoughts.

Then in 1831 a terrible disease broke out in Hamburg. It was cholera! Cholera is spread by rats and by people who live in crowded, damp, dark houses. Cholera was all the more terrible in Amalie's time because there were no hospitals for the poor. Everyone was supposed to look out for himself.

"How can I help?" thought Amalie. She wrote an article for the newspaper, calling for women to help nurse the sick. No one answered it. Amalie decided that she would do something herself, and Madame Brunnemann encouraged her. Amalie's friends were shocked when she went alone to the "hospital" which the town officials opened for the poor. They were shocked because in those days there were no women nurses. "That is so . . . unladylike," Amalie's friends said. And nothing could be worse, they thought, than for a woman to be unladylike!

The doctors did not want Amalie, either. They thought she would be more of a bother than a help. Besides, they expected her soon to get tired and leave. But when the first woman patient was carried into the hospital, the doctors sent for Amalie. Packing her things and kissing her adopted mother goodbye, Amalie went to the hospital to help during the epidemic.

Not even the housekeeper in the hospital dared come near the ward where Amalie took care of two sick women. She worked day and night to help them. The doctors watched and expected Amalie either to faint (as proper women often did) or to pick up and leave. Instead they saw her manage the sickroom as if she had done it all her life.

One day they asked Amalie to take over the men's ward, too. She was astonished. "But the men won't do as I say," she exclaimed.

"We'll see that they obey you," the doctors assured her.

The men soon grew used to seeing Amalie walk into their room quietly every few hours, day and night. She saw to it that they had clean beds and better food. They got their medicine at the right time. This was a big change, for in those days many caretakers in this hospital were dirty old men who could not do any other work. They were drunk most of the time. Some could not even read the labels on the medicine bottles! Amalie dismissed some and helped train the others.

Finally the epidemic was over. Amalie packed her suitcase to go home. She was ready to put on her bonnet when

she heard a knock at the door. Five men filed in. One of
the doctors cleared his throat and made a little speech of
thanks.

Amalie told her aunt about this and admitted she was
pleased. But what was she expected to do now? Sit at
home and be ladylike and do nothing but embroider?

Witness in Will and Deed

Amalie had begun doing some "unladylike" things. She
knew now that God did not want her to sit idle and forget
about the many poor people who needed help. Amalie had
thought long and hard about helping the poor. Now she
had some clear, definite ideas about how Christian women
should and must help. She knew that it would not be
enough just to give people money for coal, food, or rent.
"Poor families need someone who is interested in them as
persons, just as Jesus was interested in people," she said.
Above all, they needed spiritual help to learn to live a new
life. Amalie's new idea was simply this: "Not alms, but a
friend."

No longer was Amalie a shy, solemn, awkward woman.
She gathered twelve women and they formed an associa-
tion that was soon called "Friends of the Poor." The women
made regular weekly visits to poor families where there
was sickness or some other calamity.

As a girl, Amalie had watched her father keep careful
business records. Now she did the same. Each visitor to
the poor reported back to Amalie Sieveking and careful
records were kept. In this way the women learned how to
help families help themselves. A carpenter had lost the use
of his left arm. He could no longer use hammer and saw.

Amalie helped him learn to make rope slippers and so earn a living for his family. Amalie insisted on visiting the most difficult cases herself.

Amalie was not the first person to help the poor. People had taken baskets of food to the poor before. But what Amalie did was different. She helped poor families overcome their problems. She came as a loving, Christian friend. She helped them physically and spiritually.

The Queen of Denmark came to see Amalie's work and the two became close friends for life. Day after day, Amalie drove herself in long hours of work, hardly stopping to eat because she thought eating was a waste of time.

One thing led to another. Amalie saw how many children had no care when they were sick. "We need a hospital for children," she said. She started a hospital and persuaded two Lutheran deaconesses to come from Berlin and serve as nurses for the children.

Amalie was a changed person. Her black eyes sparkled with love and energy. She showed that a Christian must not only love people, but also find the right way to help. She had a warm heart, but clear, practical ideas.

Amalie learned how people lived in the crowded slums of Hamburg. How could anyone keep clean and healthy in such old, dark, damp houses? Amalie told other people about the crowded slums. She persuaded the city to give land on which neat, clean houses could be built for working people. At last the housing project was completed. Amalie Sieveking was astonished when everyone insisted that the new section of houses be named after her.

Amalie Sieveking was a pioneer when there were no women nurses, no visiting nurses, no social workers.

Though she was only one woman, without much money or education, she used every ability she had to serve God. In a happy faith in Jesus as her Savior she found strength for every new task. What a splendid life she lived! She showed a way for other women to serve Christ in serving the poor.

When Amalie was a little orphan girl, she wept because she thought no one loved her. When she died, she was loved by thousands because she brought the love of Christ to them.

11. Jean Frederic Oberlin

A WORK NOBODY ELSE WANTS

JEAN FREDERIC NEVER FORGOT the day he had a toothache early in 1767. He was a student in Strasbourg, France, and he had crawled into bed to keep warm in his cold attic room.

Was that a knock on the door? He raised his head and heard the knock again.

"Come in," he said in French, wondering who would climb three flights of stairs to a student's cold room.

"Pastor Stuber!" he said in surprise as the door opened. He did not know the pastor very well and wondered why he had come to see him.

At first Pastor Stuber did not tell Jean Frederic why he had come. Instead he asked questions. Oberlin lived on little money, Pastor Stuber observed. He knew something about medicine, didn't he, as well as theology? He spoke French as well as German?

"You are the man for the job," said Stuber at last.

"Job? What job?"

"I want you to take my place as pastor in Stone Valley up in the Vosges Mountains. Listen, it is a rocky valley high in the mountains. Winter lasts for six months there. The climate is so bad that my poor sick wife cannot live there any longer. That is why I must leave. The people are very poor and very ignorant. There is only one schoolmaster for the five villages, and he tends pigs in summer."

Jean Frederic had forgotten his toothache. He sat up. "But I have been appointed a chaplain in the French army. I am not free to consider this parish."

"I have not told you everything," said Stuber. "There are five villages and there is no road from one to the other. The houses are huts or caves dug into the mountain. The people can hardly raise enough food to keep alive. There is no place in all of France more needy than Stone Valley."

Oberlin sat thinking. While he had been studying to become a Lutheran pastor, he had often said to himself, "I want a place to work that nobody else wants. I want to do a work that will never be done unless I do it." Stone Valley sounded like the place.

It was easy to find someone else to serve as chaplain in the French army. On a blustery March day, Pastor Oberlin hiked up the trail to his parish high in the Vosges Mountains.

A Hard Beginning

Jean Frederic found that what Pastor Stuber had said was true. His people were so poor that some did not even have enough wooden shoes for everyone in the family. They could hardly get enough bread to eat, yet they had to pay heavy taxes, year after year.

Oberlin preached every Sunday. He explained the gospel in a way that was easy to understand. But he knew that God wanted him to help his people in other ways, too. "Let us not love in word or speech but in deed and in truth" was a word of Scripture that burned in his heart.

How could he, a penniless pastor, help his poor people?

Oberlin thought carefully. He decided that the most important thing was a good school for the children. Then in time they would be able to help themselves. Young and enthusiastic, Oberlin thought that people would be glad to accept help to build a schoolhouse. He even borrowed money from friends in Strasbourg and promised to repay it himself.

"That's not for us!" said the people of Stone Valley gruffly.

"We will have no school!"

"But why?" asked Oberlin.

The people had many reasons. When Oberlin explained one reason away, they thought of another. "A school means more taxes." "We would have to keep the building in repair." "We just don't want any help."

Oberlin might have shrugged his shoulders and said, "If they don't want help, I just won't bother." But Oberlin realized that a Christian cannot expect gratitude every time he tries to help someone.

Some unruly men thought it was time to teach the young pastor a lesson. They didn't like his preaching. It was too plain and too earnest. It made them feel uncomfortable. And he was always wanting to change things—like the fool idea of a school. They planned to catch him as he rode along a mountain trail and duck him in an icy stream.

"That will cool him off," they said to each other with loud guffaws.

Oberlin heard about the plot and went straight to the ringleader. "You don't know my horse, friends, if you think you can wet me. But to make it easier, I'll go on foot to-night." This took the fun out of the plot and the men decided to postpone it.

The new schoolhouse was built and then another one. Oberlin sent for good teachers and organized a new system of school studies for children, beginning with a kindergarten. This was years before anyone else had tried public schools for small children.

Oberlin had made a beginning, but no one said thank you.

Word and Deed

In Oberlin's time a pastor always wore a black suit with a white collar. He was always dignified. But one Monday morning the people of Stone Valley looked out of their doors in amazement. There was their pastor, walking down the trail with a pick over his shoulder.

"Do you suppose he will try to build that road he is always talking about?" they wondered.

Oberlin had indeed been talking about roads. "If we have a good road, you can take things to market and sell them," he said. But the people didn't want a road. They were afraid of anything new. Some grew angry. What business was that of a pastor, anyway? Let him stick to his Sunday sermons!

When they saw Oberlin on his way to build a road with his own hands, some followed to see what he would do.

They watched him work, digging up stones and getting ready to blast away a side of the cliff with gunpowder.

A few sneaked away and went home to get picks and shovels. By afternoon six men were working with the pastor. The next day there were twenty; the third day fifty. The men cut a road a mile and a half long along the cliff. Then they built a bridge across the creek to take the place of the stepping stones they used in summer. By the time the job was finished, the villagers said, "We always believed in a good road." They did not want to admit that they had ever been afraid of such a big undertaking.

It was no wonder that the people of Stone Valley were poor. Their soil was poor. Their fields needed fertilizer. The seeds they used were poor; their fruit trees were scrubby. This was the way it had always been. People thought that this was the way it had to be.

On their way to church, the people had to walk past two fields belonging to the parsonage. The fields were even more rocky and barren than their own mountain patches. One day passers-by noticed the pastor working in his fields. He said he was getting the ground ready for an orchard. People snickered. Any fool would know that no fruit tree could grow in that old, worn-out piece of land. A pastor should stick to his pulpit and not try to show farmers how to farm!

But the people could not resist coming back to see what would happen. The pastor worked hard. He brought in young fruit trees of the best stock he could find in France. He cared for the young trees. And in a few years the orchard was the marvel of the village. People tasted the fruit and found it finer than any they had ever known. Naturally

they asked Oberlin where they could get trees like his. Some started orchards of their own and prepared the soil just as they had seen the pastor do.

Year by year the crops in Stone Valley improved. The people had plenty to eat and enough to take to market on their new road. The children were well trained in the schools. Young persons had new jobs in the spinning mill Oberlin started. Gradually the whole mountain valley had changed.

Witness During the Revolution

Things were changing in France, too. In 1789 the French Revolution swept over the country. One of the ideas of the Revolution was to do away with all religion. Sunday was abolished as a day of rest. Under the rule of Robespierre the Christian religion was outlawed. Churches were closed. Many pastors fled from the country. But Oberlin stayed with his people in Stone Valley.

Oberlin could not be a pastor any more, so he got a mechanic's license. As a workingman he was allowed to organize a citizen's club. The "club" promptly named Oberlin as their "Public Orator," and as such he had the right to speak to the club. They had to decide on a place and time for the meetings of the club. "Why not use the former church as a place of meeting?" said Oberlin. "As for the day of meeting, we cannot meet on Monday, Wednesday, or Friday because they are market days at Strasbourg. What do you think of the old 'Sunday' at nine o'clock in the morning?"

So it was that in the days of the Revolution the people of Stone Valley met as a citizen's club in the church and listened to Oberlin, their "Public Orator." Other orators often denounced the tyrants of the day. Oberlin spoke about other tyrants—human sins, such as hatred, greed, impurity, and pride. He spoke of the best and only way to freedom from such tyrants: "repentance toward God and faith in the Lord Jesus Christ."

The authorities began to suspect the "club" in Stone Valley. One day when Oberlin was at the home of one of his people to celebrate a baptism, an officer came to arrest him. On the way to his trial the guards stopped at an inn. At the table some officials began to talk against all religion. Oberlin listened for a while, then he began to speak. He defended Christianity in such vigorous words that the guards decided to rush him to the military prison.

At that moment news came. Robespierre was dead! All prisoners were to be set free.

In Oberlin's later years the world began to hear about Stone Valley in the Vosges Mountains and the Lutheran pastor who had transformed it. France conferred on him the Legion of Honor award. A college in America was named Oberlin College in honor of him.

For the rest of his life Oberlin worked in remote Stone Valley in the Vosges Mountains, in a parish that no one else had wanted to serve. His life was a witness to the words of Jesus, "I was hungry and you gave me food, I was thirsty and you gave me drink, I was a stranger and you welcomed me, I was naked and you clothed me" (Matthew 25:35-36). Oberlin served Christ by serving his people in Stone Valley.

12. Toyohiko Kagawa

LOVE, THE LAW OF LIFE

ON CHRISTMAS EVE, 1909, two men pushed an old cart across Hand-to-Mouth Bridge in the great city of Kobe, Japan. One was a young Japanese student and the other a ragged ex-convict. In the cart were the student's books and belongings. The ragged man guided the cart into an unpaved alley, three feet wide. It was littered with garbage and stinking from open sewage. This was Shinkawa, the dirtiest and most crowded slum in Kobe. Here were jammed together the poorest of the poor, the most wretched people of the city. The tangle of dark, damp alleys was so dangerous that even the police did not go there at night.

The young man was Toyohiko Kagawa (*toh*-yoh-hee-ko kah-*gah*-wah), a student at the Presbyterian seminary. His friend, the ex-convict, had told him about a "house" which could be rented cheaply. No one wanted to live in it because neighbors said it was haunted by a man who had been murdered there. The "house" was exactly six feet

square; it had no windows, no water, no kitchen. An out-door toilet nearby served twenty families. It was hard to say whether the noise of drunken fighting or the stench of the slum was worse.

As a student, Kagawa had started preaching in the alleys of Shinkawa during afternoons and evenings. Then he would go back to his comfortable room at the seminary. Kagawa realized that he never really would understand the people of the slums and they never would understand or believe his Christian preaching unless he lived with them in the same kind of shabby "houses" they had. Christmas Eve seemed the right time to move among the poor and friendless.

Kagawa lived alone in his tiny house for only a few days. His first guest was a homeless man who was covered with sores from head to foot. Then came a man Kagawa called the Statue because he stayed motionless so that he could live on very little food. He stood on a street corner waiting for someone to offer him a job, but no one ever did.

Kagawa took him in because the Statue had no home. Next came a man who was haunted by nightmares. He had just been released from prison where he had been sent for killing a man. During the day he peddled bean-curd, but at night the ghost of the man he had killed appeared in his dreams and he shrieked with terror. "Let me stay with you, Kagawa," he pleaded.

Kagawa took him in and night after night the man fell asleep holding on to Kagawa's hand.

Kagawa took these people in and shared his floor and the watery rice which was all he could afford for food. He preached and lived the love of Jesus. By day he went to seminary classes. At night he preached on street corners. The people of the slum got to know him well. Some of them loved him, others laughed at him or in an angry mood broke up his meetings. Some were sure Kagawa must have money and came to his room demanding it at knife point. Kagawa never fought back. His front teeth were knocked out. He gave up the little money he had when necessary and fled when he could. He ran away from the fights, but he always came back again, preaching and helping people whenever and wherever he could.

Kagawa rented two more houses and took out the partitions to make one big room where he could hold meetings and where he could shelter homeless people. One day an old ragpicker whom everyone called the "Woman of the Cats" because she kept a dozen of them, said to Kagawa, "I have no son to care for me, to bury me when I die, and to say the prayers."

"I will be your son," said Kagawa and began to care for her, too.

Becoming a Christian

Kagawa could hardly remember his own parents because they had died when he was four years old. For a while he had lived on the family farm with his grandmother. His childhood there was spent in tears. There was no love or kindness in that home. His oldest brother soon used up the family fortune in drinking and gambling. Then Kagawa was taken into the home of his oldest uncle and sent to school. It seemed possible that the boy could make a great career in government service, but something happened that changed Kagawa.

The young student began going to the home of an American missionary to study the English language. There he also learned to believe in the Lord Jesus Christ. He met another missionary named Dr. Myers, whom he learned to love. He spent many hours reading the books in Dr. Myers' library and talking with him. Kagawa decided to become a Christian minister. When he told his uncle about this decision, his uncle flew into a rage and turned Kagawa out of the house.

Dr. Myers was ready to help Kagawa and found a place for him at the seminary. It was then that Kagawa began to preach in the slums. The long hours of reading and study, after the hard work of preaching in the filthy slums, gradually exhausted the young student. He came down with tuberculosis. After weeks in a hospital he went to the seashore to try to get back his health.

For a year Kagawa lived in an abandoned hut in a fishing village, resting and reading and remembering his childhood. The years before his father died, the time on the family farm, the days in school—why these were the materials for a novel! Now Kagawa began to write. Since he was too poor to buy paper, he wrote his story with heavy brush strokes over the printed lines of old magazines. When it was finished he copied it out on clean paper. But no publisher would print it.

Friend of Children

When Kagawa was well enough to try seminary life again, he went back to the seminary. Then on Christmas Eve, 1909, he moved into the slums and began sharing the love of Christ with people who had been cast out by everyone else. At one time there were sixteen people living with him. All depended on Kagawa for their food. One was an orphan boy named Matsuzo. Matsuzo had been one of a gang of bad boys who came when Kagawa was holding services and made noise to disturb the prayers.

The little children in the slums loved Kagawa. They would wait for him to come home from the seminary. When he was inside trying to study, the children would stand at the doorway waiting for him to come out again.

"Sensei, come play with us," they would plead.

Kagawa would come out and play games with them. One wonderful day he took the children to the seashore for a holiday. Some of his friends helped him. First they brought a big tub to the house and gave the children a bath. They scrubbed them until they were so clean they hardly knew themselves! Then they put on clean clothes and the whole party took a train ride to the shore. It was a day the children never forgot.

But often the people Kagawa helped seemed no better off than before. The orphan boy Matsuzo wavered between

good and bad. He wanted to please Kagawa, but all his life he had known unkindness and dishonesty. He couldn't understand why it was wrong to steal if he didn't get caught.

Kagawa soon came to see that it was not enough to help people after they were down and out. Something must be done to help them earlier, when they could still learn to help themselves.

How to do it? Where to begin?

Kagawa thought long and hard about these questions. He refused to be discouraged, but he found no answer.

Witnessing to a Nation

One day an editor came to visit Kagawa, hoping to write a newspaper story about his work in the slums. While they talked, Kagawa showed him the manuscript of the novel he had written at the seashore and worked on since then. The editor took it with him and published it in the newspaper.

Almost overnight, Kagawa became a famous writer. His novel was published as a book. Kagawa used the money from this book and others he wrote to do more work in the slums. It was one answer to his prayers.

Kagawa started a night school and then a medical clinic. He had been preaching early in the mornings to the dock workers and they liked and trusted him. When some of the workers came to him and asked him to help them organize a labor union, Kagawa saw this as one answer to their big problem of poverty.

Kagawa promised to help, but he believed in using only peaceful methods. Not all the men agreed with him. The police came and tried to break up the union. Kagawa was thrown into jail. In jail he began to plan another novel, using a piece of charcoal to write ideas down on scraps of wastepaper.

Kagawa became a Christian leader with new ideas and new ways to act. His love was great for all who were in need. He remembered his childhood on the farm and thought about Japanese farmers. They worked long hours and were always in debt. He saw that the farmers did not use up-to-date methods or tools. They did not make good use of the hillsides, and so much of Japan is hillside. Kagawa helped organize farmers' unions so that the farmers could work together for a better living. He worked to open new schools where farmers could learn new ways of farming, new ways of cleanliness and health.

The nation of Japan slowly came to realize that Toyohiko Kagawa, working in the slums of Kobe, starting labor unions, helping farmers, was a great man. When a terrible earthquake struck Tokyo, he was asked to serve on the relief commission. Then the mayor asked him to work as director of the Social Welfare Bureau. Kagawa's reputation grew until he became one of the best-known Christian leaders in the world.

Witness of a Christian Poet

Then Japan went to war against China. Kagawa knew that his nation was doing wrong and said so openly and boldy. Now the people who had been praising him as a new Francis of Assisi began to call him a traitor. "Kill Kagawa, the traitor!" was scrawled on posters all over the city. One day, after he had preached a sermon on peace,

Kagawa was taken to jail. When he was released from jail a short time later, he went on working for peace.

When Japan went to war against the United States, Kagawa was arrested again. He was released but was ordered to keep quiet as long as the war lasted. All the books he had written were forbidden. Kagawa was not allowed to keep on with his work for the poor. He went to live in a rest home he had founded for sick people on an island in the Inland Sea. Here he helped the patients and wrote poems in his diary.

> Not fighting only—
> Love, too, means
> Adventure.
> Nurses go bravely forth to nurse
> Cases that may mean death;
> Firemen do not flee
> The raging flames . . .
> Peace means adventure, too . . .
> The campaign of the Crucifixion
> Means adventure,
> Now and always . . .
> Let every one of us
> Rush gladly in,
> And brave the wildness
> Of the awful storm!

When the war was over, the Japanese nation turned to Kagawa again. The first public visit the emperor made was to Kagawa. To the day of his death Kagawa's life was a poem of love and sacrifice. In Kagawa's life the people of Japan could see the love and sacrifice of Jesus for all people. He showed that for a Christian love is the law of life.

13. Frank Laubach

EACH ONE TEACH ONE

In 1915, when he was thirty years old, Frank Laubach and his wife went to the Philippine Islands as missionaries. Since that time, things like radio, TV, and jet planes have changed the world greatly. But what Frank Laubach did brought even bigger changes into the lives of millions of people around the world. It began one evening on the top of Signal Hill on the Philippine island of Mindanao.

FRANK LAUBACH WHISTLED for his dog Tip and started out on his evening walk. Tip knew where they were going and darted ahead until he seemed to be only a tiny black spot on the path. When Laubach reached the top of Signal Hill, Tip sat there, waiting for him.

The missionary stood still and looked far out across the mountains, beyond the lakes, to the distant sea. Everything glowed in the golden light of sunset. It was beautiful—a sight to make a Christian burst out singing in praise to the Creator. But tonight Laubach was too unhappy to sing, even at the sight of hill and lake and sea.

Frank Laubach had come to the Philippines as a missionary to the Moro people of the island of Mindanao. Most of the Moro people were Moslems. When Laubach first came to Mindanao, he was turned away because the island was a danger zone. The outlaws in the hills attacked strangers and hated anyone who was a Christian. So Laubach went back to the city of Manila where he taught at a seminary.

In December, 1929, Frank Laubach came back to Mindanao to try again. He wanted to start a school to train teachers. But this seemed impossible also because most of the Moro people could not yet read or write.

What was even more discouraging was the ill will of the Moro people. They frowned at him in the street. When he tried to start a conversation, they would not answer. When he went into their shops, they turned away from him. What was wrong? Laubach had come to help the Moro people in Mindanao. He knew they needed the help he could give them, but if they were unwilling and angry with him . . .

"O Lord God," Frank Laubach prayed on top of Signal Hill. His mind reached out for help and there came an answer! God spoke to him through his thoughts.

"My child, you have failed because you do not really love the Moro people. You feel superior."

That is true, thought Laubach. No wonder I have failed. If I would go to the Moro people humbly—to learn—to learn about their religion . . .

First Success Among the Moros

The next day Laubach went to a *pandita,* or Moslem priest. He told him that he wanted to study the Koran, which is the Bible of the Moslems. What a change in the *pandita!* He turned eagerly to Laubach and began to tell him in broken Spanish about the holy books of the Moslems. They were four—the Law of Moses, the Psalms of David, the Gospel of Jesus, and the Koran of Mohammed.

Dr. Laubach answered in Spanish, "From childhood I have studied the first three books you name."

At once there was something to discuss. But it is hard to discuss anything, especially religion, if you do not know the language well. Laubach realized he had to study Maranaw, the language of the Moro people.

Laubach found a teacher, a Moro man named Pambaya, but when they sat down to study, they had no dictionary, in fact no books at all. Not a page of the Maranaw language had ever been printed. The *panditas* read the Koran in Arabic, but no one had ever bothered to put the Maranaw language into writing.

Dr. Laubach decided that first of all he and Pambaya would make a dictionary. That was not easy because no one knew where one Maranaw word stopped and the next one began. Only by talking with Pambaya and finding each word could Laubach make a beginning. Then he wrote each word on a separate card. After six weeks, he and Pambaya had a box filled with cards for 1300 Maranaw words and their meanings.

All the while, Laubach had many opportunities to talk about the "Gospel of Jesus" along with conversation about the Moslem religion.

Once the dictionary was finished, Laubach was ready to print a story paper in the Maranaw language. It was printed in Arabic letters on one side and English letters on the other.

Everyone was eager to see this first paper. But the only person who could read the side in English letters was Pambaya. At once all the young men wanted Laubach to teach them to read. They asked for a school in the evening. Quickly, Laubach and his helpers set up a school. They borrowed a hand printing set and printed charts in large letters. They made the sentences short and easy, like the ones in a first-grade reader. But learning to read this way was very slow work. There ought to be an easier way, thought Laubach.

Laubach and his helpers made a new chart. First they printed the name of a town, *Malabanga,* which every Moro knew. The learner could quickly understand that the letters stood for a word he knew—Ma-la-ba-nga. Then the letters in this word could be used to make new words:

> *ma-ma* means man *ma-la* means large
> *a-ma* means father *a-la* means God

In one hour a man who could not read before learned to read a whole page of words in his own language! He was delighted. Other people heard about this and asked to be taught to read.

One man came from a distant village and learned to read so quickly that Laubach praised him. The man was so happy that he took Laubach aside where no one could hear and said, "You taught me to read, and you are my best friend. Now, is there anybody in Mindanao you want me to put out of the way?"

"No, thank you, brother," said Laubach. "But you are certainly a very big-hearted man. Go home and teach others and that will make me happy."

Each One Teach One

More and more people came to Laubach's school, but soon Laubach's money was used up. No more money could be expected because there was a depression in the United States. Laubach knew he would have to close the school soon.

"This teaching must not stop because there is no money for teachers," frowned the chief. "Everybody who learns to read must teach somebody else. If he doesn't, I'll kill him!"

The chief's angry words gave Laubach a wonderful idea. "Everybody who learns must teach!" That was the answer. Then knowing how to read would spread like a prairie fire. Besides, teaching someone else would help the teacher remember what he had learned.

Laubach put the new idea into four words: *Each one teach one.* People in other countries heard about Laubach's new idea and new methods. Calls came from India, from Egypt, from many other parts of the world where there are millions of men and women who had never learned to read. "Come and help us start your teaching in our country," people asked.

On his way home for a visit, Laubach did just that. He traveled a roundabout way that took him to India and Egypt and other places that wanted his help.

Sometimes Laubach failed. No matter how good his new language charts might be, he learned that it is more important to have the right kind of teachers—people who are patient, humble, and encouraging. New learners often feel shy and ashamed because they cannot read. Teachers must not let their pupils fail, but should help and praise them for every little thing that they do right.

"Never scold or frown," said Laubach. "Pat the student on the back and tell him how bright he is. Treat him like a rajah."

Laubach worked hard to make better language charts. He noticed that people who do not read usually notice the shapes of things. If a chart had pictures, they could think of the right sounds for each letter more quickly. For example, the *picture* for the "S" sound in English might be a snake because an "S" shape looks like a snake. Besides the hissing sound of the letter "S" makes one think of a snake.

Now Laubach made charts with a picture for each letter of the alphabet. People could learn very rapidly by looking at the pictures and comparing them to the letters of the alphabet.

Dr. Laubach helped other missionaries use his new ideas. Governments became interested. Soon great learn-to-read campaigns were under way in Africa and India, Burma and Ceylon, South America and many other countries where people had not learned to read.

In one of his books Laubach wrote, "A man who cannot read is like a blind man." Laubach helped open the reading eyes of millions of people. He taught Christian missionaries how to write down languages that never had been written down before, how to translate books of the Bible into new languages, how to make picture charts for new languages. He wrote a simple story of Jesus which missionaries have used in many languages.

Because people are hungry for books to read, many Christian men and women are now busy writing easy-to-understand books for people who have just learned to read: books to help mothers take care of babies, books to help farmers improve their fields, and especially books to help people know the will and love of God.

As Laubach traveled from country to country, there was one thing he always wanted to talk about. He never could forget that evening long ago on Signal Hill. He loved to tell how God was answering his prayer in ways more wonderful than he ever had imagined. Everywhere Laubach went, he tried to help people learn to read. Then they could read the witness to Christ in the Bible themselves. And what was very important, he wanted them to learn about prayer and the great power of God to help.